||||| ||||||||||||||||||||||
D1072221

ADVENTURES IN THE ARTS

ADVENTURES
IN THE ARTS

**INFORMAL
CHAPTERS
ON PAINTERS
VAUDEVILLE
AND POETS**

BY

MARSDEN HARTLEY

HACKER ART BOOKS

NEW YORK

1972

First published by Boni and Liveright, Inc.
New York, 1921
Reprinted by Hacker Art Books, Inc.
New York, 1972

Library of Congress Catalog Card Number: 78-143351
ISBN: 0-87817-071-5

PREFATORY NOTE

The papers in this book are not intended in any way to be professional treatises. They must be viewed in the light of entertaining conversations. Their possible value lies in their directness of impulse, and not in weight of argument. I could not wish to go into the qualities of art more deeply. A reaction, to be pleasant, must be simple. This is the apology I have to offer: Reactions, then, through direct impulse, and not essays by means of stiffened analysis.

MARSDEN HARTLEY.

Some of the papers included in this book have appeared in *Art and Archeology*, *The Seven Arts*, *The Dial*, *The Nation*, *The New Republic*, and *The Touchstone*. Thanks are due to the editors of these periodicals for permission to reprint.

TO
ALFRED STIEGLITZ

INTRODUCTION
TO
ADVENTURES IN THE ARTS

PERHAPS the most important part of Criticism is the fact that it presents to the creator a problem which is never solved. Criticism is to him a perpetual Presence: or perhaps a ghost which he will not succeed in laying. If he could satisfy his mind that Criticism was a certain thing: a good thing or a bad, a proper presence or an irrelevant, he could psychologically dispose of it. But he can not. For Criticism is a configuration of responses and reactions so intricate, so kaleidoscopic, that it would be as simple to category Life itself.

The artist remains the artist precisely in so far as he rejects the simplifying and reducing process of the average man who at an early age puts Life away into some snug conception of his mind and race. This one turns the key. He has released his will and love from the vast Ceremonial of wonder, from the deep Poem of Being, into some particular detail of life wherein he hopes to achieve comfort or at least shun pain. Not so, the artist. In the moment when he elects to avoid by whatever makeshift the raw agony of life, he ceases to be fit to create. He must face experience forever freshly: reduce life each day anew to chaos and remould it into order. He must be always a willing virgin, given up to life and so enlacing it. Thus only may he retain and record that pure surprise whose earliest voicing is the first cry of the infant.

The unresolved expectancy of the creator toward Life should be his way toward Criticism also. He should hold it as part of his Adventure. He should understand in it, particularly when it is impertinent, stupid and cruel, the ponderable weight of Life itself, reacting upon his search for a fresh conquest over it. Though it persist unchanged in its rôle of purveying misinformation and absurdity to the Public, he should know it for himself a blessed dispensation.

With his maturity, the creator's work goes out into the world. And in this act, he puts the world away. For the artist's work defines: and definition means apartness: and the average man is undefined in the social body. Here is a danger for the artist within the very essence of his artistic virtue. During the years of his apprenticeship, he has struggled to create for himself an essential world out of experience. Now he begins to succeed: and he lives too fully in his own selection: he lives too simply in the effects of his effort. The gross and fumbling impact of experience is eased. The grind of ordinary intercourse is dimmed. The rawness of Family and Business is refined or removed. But now once more the world comes in to him, in the form of the Critic. Here again, in a sharp concentrated sense, the world moves on him: its complacency, its hysteria, its down-tending appetites and fond illusions, its pathetic worship of yesterdays and hatred of tomorrows, its fear-dogmas and its blood-avowals.

The artist shall leave the world only to find it, hate it only because he loves, attack it only if he serves. At that epoch of his life when the world's gross sources may grow dim, Criticism brings them back. Wherefore, the function of the Critic is a blessing and a need.

The creator's reception of this newly direct, intense, mundane intrusion is not always passive. If the artist is an intelligent man, he may respond to the intervening world on its own plane. He may turn critic himself.

When the creator turns critic, we are in the presence of a consummation: we have a complete experience: we have a sort of sacrament. For to the intrusion of the world he interposes his own body. In his art, the creator's body would be itself intrusion. The artist is too humble and too sane to break the ecstatic flow of vision with his personal form. The true artist despises the personal as an end. He makes fluid, and distils his personal form. He channels it beyond himself to a Unity which of course contains it. But Criticism is nothing which

INTRODUCTION

is not the sheer projection of a body. The artist
turns Self into a universal Form: but the critic re-
duces Form to Self. Criticism is to the artist the
intrusion, in a form irreducible to art, of the body
of the world. What can he do but interpose his
own?

This is the value of the creator's criticism. He
gives to the world himself. And his self is a rich
life.

It includes for instance a direct experience of art,
the which no professional critic may possess. And
it includes as well a direct knowledge of life, sharp-
ened in the retrospect of that devotion to the living
which is peculiarly the artist's. For what is the
critic after all, but an "artistic" individual somehow
impeded from satisfying his esthetic emotion and
his need of esthetic form in the gross and stubborn
stuff of life itself: who therefore, since he is too
intelligent for substitutes, resorts to the already
digested matter of the hardier creators, takes their
assimilated food and does with it what the athletic
artist does with the meat and lymph and bone of
God himself? The artist mines from the earth and
smelts with his own fire. He is higher brother to
the toilers of the soil. The critic takes the prod-
ucts of the creator, reforges, twists them, always in
the cold. For if he had the fire to melt, he would
not stay with metals already worked: when the
earth's womb bursts with richer.

When the creator turns critic, we are certain of

xiv

INTRODUCTION

a feast. We have a fare that needs no metaphysical sauce (such as must transform the product of the Critic). Here is good food. Go to it and eat. The asides of a Baudelaire, a Goethe, a Da Vinci outweight a thousand tomes of the professional critics.

I know of no American book like this one by Marsden Hartley. I do not believe American painting heretofore capable of so vital a response and of so athletic an appraisal. Albert Ryder barricaded himself from the world's intrusion. The American world was not intelligent enough in his days to touch him to an activer response. And Ryder, partaking of its feebleness, from his devotion to the pure subjective note became too exhausted for aught else. As a world we have advanced. We have a fully functioning Criticism . . . swarms and schools of makers of the sonorous complacencies of Judgment. We have an integral body of creative-minded men and women interposing itself with valiance upon the antithesis of the social resistance to social growth. Hartley is in some ways a continuance of Ryder. One stage is Ryder, the solitary who remained one. A second stage is Hartley, the solitary who stands against the more aggressive, more interested Marketplace.

You will find in this book the artist of a cultural epoch. This man has mastered the plastic mes-

INTRODUCTION

sages of modern Europe: he has gone deep in the classic forms of the ancient Indian Dance. But he is, still, not very far from Ryder. He is always the child—whatever wise old worlds he contemplates —the child, wistful, poignant, trammeled, of New England.

Hartley has adventured not alone deep but wide. He steps from New Mexico to Berlin, from the salons of the Paris of Marie Laurencin to the dust and tang of the American Circus. He is eclectic. But wherever he goes he chronicles not so much these actual worlds as his own pleasure of them. They are but mirrors, many-shaped and lighted, for his own delicate, incisive humor. For Hartley is an innocent and a *naïf*. At times he is profound. Always he is profoundly simple.

Tragedy and Comedy are adult. The child's world is Tragicomic. So Marsden Hartley's. He is not deep enough—like most of our Moderns— in the pregnant chaos to be submerged in blackness by the hot struggle of the creative will. He may weep, but he can smile next moment at a pretty song. He may be hurt, but he gets up to dance.

In this book—the autobiography of a creator— Marsden Hartley peers variously into the modern world: but it is in search of Fairies.

WALDO FRANK.

Lisbon, June, 1921.

CONTENTS

xvii

CONTENTS

FOREWORD

CONCERNING FAIRY TALES
AND ME

SOMETIMES I think myself one of the unique children among children. I never read a fairy story in my childhood. I always had the feeling as a child, that fairy stories were for grown-ups and were best understood by them, and for that reason I think it must have been that I postponed them. I found them, even at sixteen, too involved and mystifying to take them in with quite the simple gullibility that is necessary. But that was because I was left alone with the incredibly magical reality from morning until nightfall, and the nights meant nothing more remarkable to me than the days did, no more than they do now. I find moonlight merely another species of illumination by which one registers continuity of sensation. My nursery was always on the edge of the strangers' knee, wondering who they were, what they might even mean to those who were as is called "nearest" them.

I had a childhood vast with terror and surprise. If it is true that one forgets what one wishes to forget, then I have reason for not remembering the major part of those days and hours that are supposed to introduce one graciously into the world and offer one a clue to the experience that is sure to follow. Not that my childhood was so bitter, unless for childhood loneliness is bitterness, and without doubt it is the worst thing that can happen to one's childhood. Mine was merely a different childhood, and in this sense an original one. I was left with myself to discover myself amid the multitudinous other and far greater mysteries. I was never the victim of fear of goblins and ghosts because I was never taught them. I was merely taught by nature to follow, as if led by a rare and tender hand, the then almost unendurable beauty that lay on every side of me. It was pain then, to follow beauty, because I didn't understand beauty; it must always, I think, be distressing to follow anything one does not understand.

I used to go, in my earliest school days, into a little strip of woodland not far from the great ominous red brick building in a small manufacturing town, on the edge of a wonderful great river in Maine, from which cool and quiet spot I could always hear the dominant clang of the bell, and there I could listen with all my very boyish simplicity to the running of the water over the stones, and watch—for it was spring, of course—the new leaves pushing up out of the mould, and see the light-hued blossoms swinging on the new breeze. I cared more for these in themselves than I did for any legendary presences sitting under them, shaking imperceptible fingers and waving invisible wands

4

with regality in a world made only for them and for children who were taught mechanically to see them there.

I was constantly confronted with the magic of reality itself, wondering why one thing was built of exquisite curves and another of harmonic angles. It was not a scientific passion in me, it was merely my sensing of the world of visible beauty around me, pressing in on me with the vehemence of splendor, on every side.

I feel about the world now precisely as I did then, despite all the reasons that exist to encourage the change of attitude. I care for the magic of experience still, the magic that exists even in facts, though little or nothing for the objective material value.

Life as an idea engrosses me with the same ardor as in the earlier boyish days, with the difference that there is much to admire and so much less to reverence and be afraid of. I harp always on the "idea" of life as I dwell perpetually on the existence of the moment.

I might say, then, that my childhood was comparable, in its simplicity and extravagance of wonder, to the youth of Odilon Redon, that remarkable painter of the fantasy of existence, of which he speaks so delicately in letters to friends. His youth was apparently much like mine, not a youth of athleticism so much as a preoccupancy with wonder and the imminence of beauty surrounding all things.

CONCERNING FAIRY TALES

I was preoccupied with the "being" of things. Things in themselves engrossed me more than the problem of experience. I was satisfied with the effect of things upon my senses, and cared nothing for their deeper values. The inherent magic in the appearance of the world about me, engrossed and amazed me. No cloud or blossom or bird or human ever escaped me, I think.

I was not indifferent to anything that took shape before me, though when it came to people I was less credulous of their perfection because they pressed forward their not always certain credentials upon me. I reverenced them then too much for an imagined austerity as I admire them now perhaps not enough for their charm, for it is the charm of things and people only that engages and satisfies me. I have completed my philosophical equations, and have become enamored of people as having the same propensities as all other objects of nature. One need never question appearances. One accepts them for their face value, as the camera accepts them, without recommendation or specialized qualification. They are what they become to one. The capacity for legend comes out of the capacity for experience, and it is in this fashion that I hold such high respect for geniuses like Grimm and Andersen, but as I know their qualities I find myself leaning with more readiness toward Lewis Carroll's superb "Alice in Wonderland."

I was, I suppose, born backward, physically

speaking. I was confronted with the vastitude of
the universe at once, without the ingratiating introduction of the fairy tale. I had early made the
not so inane decision that I would not read a book
until I really wanted to. One of the rarest women
in the world, having listened to my remark, said
she had a book she knew I would like because it
was so different, and forthwith presented me with
Emerson's Essays, the first book that I have any
knowledge of reading, and it was in my eighteenth
year. Until then I had been wholly absorbed with
the terrors and the majestical inferences of the moment, the hour, and the day. I was alone with them,
and they were wonderful and excessively baffling in
their splendors; then, after filling my mind and soul
with the legendary splendors of Friendship, and
The Oversoul-Circles, and Compensation, each of
these words of exciting largeness in themselves, I
turned to the dramatic unrealities of Zarathustra,
which, of course, was in no way to be believed because it did not exist. And then came expansion
and release into the outer world again through interpretation of Plato, and of Leaves of Grass itself.

I have saved myself from the disaster of beliefs
through these magical books, and am free once
more as in my early childhood to indulge myself
in the iridescent idea of life, as Idea.

But the fairy story is nothing after all but a
means whereby we, as children, may arrive at some
clue as to the significance of things around us, and

it is through them the child finds his way out from incoherency toward comprehension. The universe is a vast place, as we all know who think we comprehend it in admiring it. The things we cannot know are in reality of no consequence, in comparison with the few we can know. I can know, for instance, that my morning is the new era of my existence, and that I shall never live through another like it, as I have never lived through the one I recall in my memory, which was Yesterday. Yesterday was my event in experience then, as it is my event in memory now. I am related to the world by the way I feel attached to the life of it as exemplified in the vividness of the moment. I am, by reason of my peculiar personal experience, enabled to extract the magic from the moment, discarding the material husk of it precisely as the squirrel does the shell of the nut.

I am preoccupied with the business of transmutation—which is to say, the proper evaluation of life as idea, of experience as delectable diversion. It is necesary for everyone to poetize his sensations in order to comprehend them. Weakness in the direction of philosophy creates the quality of dogmatic interrogation. A preoccupancy with religious characteristics assists those who are interested in the problem of sublimation. The romanticist is a kind of scientific person engaged in the correct assembling of chemical constituents that will produce a formula by which he can live out every one of his

8

moments with a perfect comprehension of their charm and of their everlasting value to him. If the romanticist have the advantage of comprehension of the sense of beauty as related to art, then he may be said to be wholly equipped for the exquisite legend of life in which he takes his place, as factor in the perfected memory of existence, which becomes the real history of life, as an idea. The person of most power in life is he who becomes high magician with the engaging and elusive trick.

It is a fairy-tale in itself if you will, and everyone is entitled to his or her own private splendor, which, of course, must be invented from intelligence for oneself.

There will be no magic found away from life. It is what you do with the street-corner in your brain that shall determine your gift. It will not be found in the wilderness, and in one's toying with the magic of existence is the one gift for the management of experience.

I hope one day, when life as an "idea" permits, and that I have figured will be somewhere around my ninetieth year, to take up books that absorb the brains of the intelligent. When I read a book, it is because it will somehow expose to me the magic of existence. My fairy tales of late have been "Wuthering Heights," and the work of the Brothers James, Will and Henry. I am not so sure but that I like William best, and I assure you that is

9

saying a great deal, but it is only because I think William is more like life as idea.

I shall hope when it comes time to sit in a garden and fold one's hands gently, listening to the birds all over again, watching the blossoms swinging with a still acuter eye, to take up the books of Grimm and Andersen, for I have a feeling they will be the books that will best corroborate my comprehension of life as an idea. I think it will be the best time to read them then, to go out with a memory softened by the warm hues and touches of legend that rise out of the air surrounding life itself.

There will be a richer comprehension of "once upon a time there was a princess"—who wore a great many jewelled rings on her fingers and whose eyes were like deep pools in the farthest fields of the sky—for that will be the lady who let me love in the ways I was made to forget; the lady whose hands I have touched as gently as possible and from whom I have exacted no wish save that I might always love someone or something that was so like herself as to make me think it was no other than herself. It is because I love the idea of life better than anything else that I believe most of all in the magic of existence, and in spite of much terrifying and disillusioning experience of late, I *believe*.

PART ONE

THE RED MAN

It is significant that all races, and primitive peoples especially, exhibit the wish somehow to inscribe their racial autograph before they depart. It is our redman who permits us to witness the signing of his autograph with the beautiful gesture of his body in the form of the symbolic dance which he and his forefathers have practiced through the centuries, making the name America something to be remembered among the great names of the world and of time. It is the redman who has written down our earliest known history, and it is of his symbolic and esthetic endeavors that we should be most reasonably proud. He is the one man who has shown us the significance of the poetic aspects of our original land. Without him we should still be unrepresented in the cultural development of the world. The wide discrepancies between our earliest history and our present make it an imperative issue for everyone loving the name America to cherish him while he remains among us as the only esthetic representative of our great country up to the present hour. He has indicated for all time the symbolic splendor of our plains, canyons, mountains, lakes, mesas and ravines, our forests and our native skies, with their animal

13

inhabitants, the buffalo, the deer, the eagle and the various other living presences in their midst. He has learned throughout the centuries the nature of our soil and has symbolized for his own religious and esthetic satisfaction all the various forms that have become benefactors to him.

Americans of this time and of time to come shall know little or nothing of their spacious land until they have sought some degree of intimacy with our first artistic relative. The redman is the one truly indigenous religionist and esthete of America. He knows every form of animal and vegetable life adhering to our earth, and has made for himself a series of striking pageantries in the form of stirring dances to celebrate them, and his relation to them. Throughout the various dances of the Pueblos of the Rio Grande those of San Felipe, Santo Domingo, San Ildefonso, Taos, Tesuque, and all the other tribes of the west and the southwest, the same unified sense of beauty prevails, and in some of the dances to a most remarkable degree. For instance, in a large pueblo like Santo Domingo, you have the dance composed of nearly three hundred people, two hundred of whom form the dance contingent, the other third a chorus, probably the largest singing chorus in the entire redman population of America. In a small pueblo like Tesuque, the theme is beautifully represented by from three to a dozen individuals, all of them excellent performers in various ways. The same quality and the same character, the same sense of beauty, prevails in all of them.

It is the little pueblo of Tesuque which has just finished its series of Christmas dances—a four-day festival celebrating with all but impeccable mastery the various identities which have meant so much to them both physically and spiritually—that I would here cite as an example. It is well known that once gesture is organized, it requires but a handful of people to represent multitude; and this lonely handful of redmen in the pueblo of Tesuque, numbering at most but seventy-five or eighty individuals, lessened, as is the case with all the pueblos of the country to a tragical degree by the recent invasions of the influenza epidemic, showed the interested observer, in groups of five or a dozen dancers and soloists including drummers, through the incomparable pageantry of the buffalo, the eagle, the snowbird, and other varying types of small dances, the mastery of the redman in the art of gesture, the art of symbolized pantomimic expression. It is the buffalo, the eagle, and the deer dances that show you their essential greatness as artists. You find a species of rhythm so perfected in its relation to racial interpretation as hardly to admit of witnessing ever again the copied varieties of dancing such as we whites of the present hour are familiar with. It is nothing short of captivating artistry of first excellence, and we are familiar with nothing that equals it outside the Negro syncopation which we now know so well, and from which we have borrowed all we have of native expression.

If we had the redman sense of time in our system, we would be better able to express ourselves. We are notoriously unorganized in esthetic conception, and what we appreciate most is merely the athletic phase of bodily expression, which is of course attractive enough, but is not in itself a formal mode of expression. The redman would teach us to be ourselves in a still greater degree, as his forefathers have taught him to be himself down the centuries, despite every obstacle. It is now as the last obstacle in the way of his racial expression that we as his host and guardian are pleasing ourselves to figure. It is as inhospitable host we are quietly urging denunciation of his pagan ceremonials. It is an inhospitable host that we are, and it is amazing enough, our wanting to suppress him. You will travel over many continents to find a more beautifully synthesized artistry than our redman offers. In times of peace we go about the world seeking out every species of life foreign to ourselves for our own esthetic or intellectual diversion, and yet we neglect on our very doorstep the perhaps most remarkable realization of beauty that can be found anywhere. It is of a perfect piece with the great artistry of all time. We have to go for what we know of these types of expression to books and to fragments of stone, to monuments and to the preserved bits of pottery we now may see under glass mostly, while there is the living remnant of a culture so fine in its appreciation of the beauty of things, under our own home eye, so near that we can not even see it.

A glimpse of the buffalo dance alone will furnish proof sufficient to you of the sense of symbolic significances in the redman that is unsurpassed. The redman is a genius in his gift of masquerade alone. He is a genius in detail, and in ensemble, and the producer of today might learn far more from him than he can be aware of except by visiting his unique performances. The redman's notion of the theatric does not depend upon artificial appliances. He relies entirely upon the sun with its so clear light of the west and southwest to do his profiling and silhouetting for him, and he knows the sun will co-operate with every one of his intentions. He allows for the sense of mass and of detail with proper proportion, allows also for the interval of escape in mood, crediting the value of the pause with the ability to do its prescribed work for the eye and ear perfectly, and when he is finished he retires from the scene carefully to the beating of the drums, leaving the emotion to round itself out gradually until he disappears, and silence completes the picture for the eye and the brain. His staging is of the simplest, and therefore, the most natural. Since he is sure of his rhythms, in every other dancer as well as himself, he is certain of his ensemble, and is likewise sure there will be no dead spots either in the scenario or in the presentation. His production is not a show for the amusement of the onlooker; it is a pageant for the edification of his own soul. Each man is therefore concerned with the staging of the idea, because it is his own spiritual drama in a state of enaction, and each is in his own way manager of the scene, and of the duos, trios, and ensembles, or whatever form the dances may require. It is therefore of a piece with his conception of nature and the struggle for realism is not necessary, since he is at all times the natural actor, the natural expresser of the indications and suggestions derived from the great theme of nature which occupies his mind, and body, and soul. His acting is invented by himself for purposes of his own, and it is nature that gives him the sign and symbol for the expression of life as a synthesis. He is a genius in plastic expression, and every movement of his is sure to register in the unity of the theme, because he himself is a powerful unit of the group in which he may be performing. He is esthetically a responsible factor, since it concerns him as part of the great idea. He is leading soloist and auxiliary in one. He is the significant instrument in the orchestration of the theme at hand, and knows his body will respond to every requirement of phrasing. You will find the infants, of two and three years of age even, responding in terms of play to the exacting rhythms of the dance, just as with orientals it was the children often who wove the loveliest patterns in their rugs.

In the instance of the buffalo dance of the Tesuque

THE RED MAN

Indians, contrary to what might be expected or would popularly be conceived, there is not riotry of color, but the costumes are toned rather in the sombre hues of the animal in question, and after the tone of the dark flanks of the mountains crested and avalanched with snows, looking more like buffaloes buried knee deep in white drifts than anything else one may think of. They bring you the sense of the power of the buffalo personality, the formidable beast that once stampeded the prairies around them, solemnized with austere gesturing, enveloping him with stateliness, and the silence of the winter that surrounds themselves. Three men, two of them impersonating the buffalo, the third with bow and arrow in hand, doubtless the hunter, and two women representing the mother buffalo, furnish the ensemble. Aside from an occasional note of red in girdles and minor trappings, with a softening touch of green in the pine branches in their hands, the adjustment of hue is essentially one of the black and white, one of the most difficult harmonies in esthetic scales the painter encounters in the making of a picture, the most difficult of all probably, by reason of its limited range and the economic severity of color. It calls for nothing short of the finest perception of nuance, and it is the redman of America who knows with an almost flawless eye the natural harmonies of the life that surrounds him. He has for so long decorated his body with the hues of the earth that he has grown to be a part of them.

He is a living embodiment in color of various tonal characteristics of the landscape around him. He knows the harmonic value of a bark or a hide, or a bit of broken earth, and of the natural unpolluted coloring to be drawn out of various types of vegetable matter at his disposal. Even if he resorts to our present-day store ribbons and cheap trinkets for accessories, he does it with a view to creating the appearance of racial ensemble. He is one of the essential decorators of the world. A look at the totem poles and the prayer robes of the Indians of Alaska will convince you of that.

In the buffalo dance, then, you perceive the red-man's fine knowledge of color relations, of the harmonizing of buffalo skins, of white buckskins painted with most expressively simple designs symbolizing the various earth identities, and the accompanying ornamentation of strings of shells and other odd bits having a black or a grey and white lustre. You get an adjusted relation of white which traverses the complete scale of color possibility in monochrome. The two men representing the buffalo, with buffalo heads covering their heads and faces from view, down to their breasts, their bodies to the waist painted black, no sign of pencillings visible to relieve the austerity of intention, legs painted black and white, with cuffs of skunk's fur round the ankles to represent the death mask symbol, relieving the edges of the buckskin moccasins—in all this you have the notes that are necessary for the color balance of the idea of solemnity presented to the eye. You find even the white starlike splashes here and there on backs, breasts and arms coinciding splendidly with the flecks of eagles-down that quiver in the wind down their black bodies, and the long black hair of the accompanying hunter, as flecks of foam would rise from waterfalls of dark mountain streams; and the feathers that float from the tips of the buffalo horns seem like young eaglets ready to leave the eyry, to swim for the first time the far fields of air above and below them, to traverse with skill the sunlit spaces their eyes have opened to with a fierce amazement. Even the clouds of frozen breath darting from the lips of the dancers served as an essential phase of the symbolic decoration, and the girdles of tiny conchlike shells rattling round their agile thighs made a music you were glad to hear. The sunshine fell from them, too, in scales of light, danced around the spaces enveloping them along with the flecks of eagle-down that floated away from their bodies with the vigors of the dance, floating away from their dark warm bodies, and their jet-blue hair. It is the incomparable understanding of their own inventive rhythms that inspire and impress you as spectator. It is the swift comprehension of change in rhythm given them by the drummers, the speedy response of their so living pulsating bodies, the irresistible rapport with the varying themes, that thrills and invites you to remain close to the picture. They know, as perfect artists would know, the essential value of the materials at their disposal, and the eye for harmonic relationships is as keen as the impeccable gift for rhythm which is theirs. The note of skill was again accentuated when, at the close of the season's ensemble with a repetition of the beautiful eagle dance, there appeared two grotesqueries in the form of charming devil spirits in the hues of animals also, again in startling arrangements of black and white, with the single hint of color in the red lips of the masks that covered their heads completely from view, and from which long tails of white horsehair fell down their grey white backs—completing the feeling once again of stout animal spirits roaming through dark forests in search of sad faces, or, it may even be, of evil doers.

All these dances form the single spectacle surviving from a great race that no American can afford actually to miss, and certainly not to ignore. It is easy to conceive with what furore of amazement these spectacles would be received if they were brought for a single performance to our metropolitan stage. But they will never be seen away from the soil on which they have been conceived and perpetuated. It is with a simple cordiality the redman permits you to witness the esthetic survivals of his great race. It is the artist and the poet for whom they seem to be almost especially created, since these are probably nearest to understanding them from the point of view of finely organized expression; for it is by the artist and the poet of the first order that they have been invented and perfected. We as Americans of today would profit by assisting as much as possible in the continuance of these beautiful spectacles, rather than to assist in the calm dismissal and destruction of them. It is the gesture of a slowly but surely passing race which they themselves can not live without; just as we, if we but knew the ineffable beauty of them, would want at least to avail ourselves of a feast for the eye which no other country in existence can offer us, and which any other nation in the world would be only too proud to cherish and foster.

We are not, I think, more than vaguely conscious of what we possess in these redman festivities, by way of esthetic prize. It is with pain that one hears rumors of official disapproval of these rare and invaluable ceremonials. Those familiar with human psychology understand perfectly that the one· necessary element for individual growth is freedom to act according to personal needs. Once an opposition of any sort is interposed, you get a blocked aspect of evolution, you get a withered branch, and it may even be a dead root. All sorts of complexes and complexities occur. You get deformity, if not complete helplessness and annihilation. I can not imagine what would happen to the redman if his one racial gesture were denied him, if he were forbidden to perform his symbolic dances from season to season. It is a survival that is as spiritually imperative to him as it is physically and emotionally necessary. I can see a whole flood of exquisite inhibitions heaped up for burial and dry rot within the caverns and the interstices of his soul. He is a rapidly disappearing splendor, despite the possible encouragement of statistics. He needs the dance to make his body live out its natural existence, precisely as he needs the air for his lungs and blood for his veins. He needs to dance as we need to laugh to save ourselves from fixed stages of morbidity and disintegration. It is the laughter of his body that he insists upon, as well as depends upon. A redman deprived of his racial gesture is unthinkable. You would have him soon the bleached carcass in the desert out of which death moans, and from which the lizard crawls. It would be in the nature of direct race suicide. He needs protection therefore rather than disapproval. It is as if you clipped the wing of the eagle, and then asked him to soar to the sun, to cut a curve on the sky with the instrument dislodged; or as if you asked the deer to roam the wood with its cloven hoofs removed. You can not cut the main artery of the body and expect it to continue functioning. Depriving the redman of his one enviable gesture would be cutting the artery of racial instinct, emptying the beautiful chamber of his soul of its enduring consciousness. The window would be opened and the bird flown to a dead sky. It is simply unthinkable. The redman is essentially a thankful and a religious being. He

24

needs to celebrate the gifts his heaven pours upon him. Without them he would in short perish, and perish rapidly, having no breath to breathe, and no further need for survival. He is already in process of disappearance from our midst, with the attempts toward assimilation.

Inasmuch as we have the evidence of a fine aristocracy among us still, it would seem as if it behooved us as a respectable host to let the redman guest entertain himself as he will, as he sublimely does, since as guardians of such exceptional charges we can not seem to entertain them. There is no logical reason why they should accept an inferior hospitality, other than with the idea of not inflicting themselves upon a strange host more than is necessary. The redman in the aggregate is an example of the peaceable and unobtrusive citizen; we would not presume to interfere with the play of children in the sunlight. They are among the beautiful children of the world in their harmlessness. They are among the aristocracy of the world in the matters of ethics, morals, and etiquette. We forget they are vastly older, and in symbolic ways infinitely more experienced than ourselves. They do not share in tailor-made customs. They do not need imposed culture, which is essentially inferior to their own. Soon we shall see them written on tablets of stone, along with the Egyptians and the others among the races that have perished. The esthetics of the redman have been too particular to permit of universal understanding, and of universal adaptation. It is the same with all primitives, who invent regimes and modes of expression for themselves according to their own specific psychological needs. We encourage every other sign and indication of beauty toward the progress of perfection. Why should not we encourage a race that is beautiful by the proof of centuries to remain the unoffensive guest of the sun and the moon and the stars while they may? As the infant prodigy among races, there is much that we could inherit from these people if we could prove ourselves more worthy and less egotistic.

The artist and the poet of perception come forward with heartiest approval and it is the supplication of the poet and the artist which the redman needs most of all. Science looks upon him as a phenomenon; esthetics looks upon him as a giant of masterful expression in our midst. The redman is poet and artist of the very first order among the geniuses of time. We have nothing more native at our disposal than the beautiful creations of this people. It is singular enough that the as yet remote black man contributes the only native representation of rhythm and melody we possess. As an intelligent race, we are not even sure we want to welcome him as completely as we might, if his color were just a shade warmer, a shade nearer our own. We have no qualms about yellow and white and the oriental intermediate hues. We may therefore accept the redman without any of the prejudices peculiar to other types of skin, and we may accept his contribution to our culture as a most significant and important one. We haven't even begun to make use of the beautiful hints in music alone which he has given to us. We need, and abjectly so I may say, an esthetic concept of our own. Other nations of the world have long since accepted Congo originality. The world has yet to learn of the originality of the redman, and we who have him as our guest, knowing little or nothing of his powers and the beauty he confers on us by his remarkable esthetic propensities, should be the first to welcome and to foster him. It is not enough to admit of archaeological curiosity. We need to admit, and speedily, the rare and excellent esthetics in our midst, a part of our own intimate scene. The redman is a spiritual expresser of very vital issues. If his pottery and his blankets offer the majority but little, his ceremonials do contribute to the comparative few who can perceive a spectacle we shall not see the equal of in history again. It would help at least a little toward proving to the world around us that we are not so young a country as we might seem, nor yet as diffident as our national attitude would seem to indicate. The smile alone of the redman is the light of our rivers, plains, canyons, and mountains. He has the calm of all our native earth. It is from the earth all things arise. It is our geography that makes us Americans of the present, chil-

27

ADVENTURES IN THE ARTS

dren. We are the product of a day. The redman is the product of withered ages. He has written and is still writing a very impressive autograph on the waste places of history. It would seem to me to be a sign of modernism in us to preserve the living esthetic splendors in our midst. Every other nation has preserved its inheritances. We need likewise to do the same. It is not enough to put the redman as a specimen under glass along with the auk and the dinosaur. He is still alive and longing to live. We have lost the buffalo and the beaver and we are losing the redman, also, and all these are fine symbols of our own native richness and austerity. The redman will perpetuate himself only by the survival of his own customs for he will never be able to accept customs that are as foreign to him as ours are and must always be; he will never be able to accept a culture which is inferior to his own.

In the esthetic sense alone, then, we have the redman as a gift. As Americans we should accept the one American genius we possess, with genuine alacrity. We have upon our own soil something to show the world as our own, while it lives. To restrict the redman now would send him to an unrighteous oblivion. He has at least two contributions to confer, a very aristocratic notion of religion, and a superb gift for stylistic expression. He is the living artist in our midst, and we need not think of him as merely the anthropological variation or as an archaeological diversion merely. He proves the importance of synthetic registration in peoples. He has created his system for himself, from substance on, through outline down to every convincing detail. We are in a position always of selecting details in the hope of constructing something usable for ourselves. It is the superficial approach. We are imitators because we have by nature or force of circumstance to follow, and improve upon, if we can. We merely "impose" something. We can not improve upon what the redman offers us in his own way. To "impose" something—that is the modern culture. The interval of imposition is our imaginary interval of creation. The primitives created a complete cosmos for themselves, an entire principle. I want merely, then, esthetic recognition in full of the contribution of the redman as artist, as one of the finest artists of time; the poetic redman ceremonialist, celebrant of the universe as he sees it, and master among masters of the art of symbolic gesture. It is pitiable to dismiss him from our midst. He needs rather royal invitation to remain and to persist, and he can persist only by expressing himself in his own natural and distinguished way, as is the case with all peoples, and all individuals, indeed.

WHITMAN AND CÉZANNE

IT is interesting to observe that in two fields of expression, those of painting and poetry, the two most notable innovators, Whitman and Cézanne bear a definite relationship in point of similarity of ideals and in their attitudes toward esthetic principles. Both of these men were so true to their respective ideals that they are worth considering at the same time in connection with each other: Cézanne with his desire to join the best that existed in the impressionistic principle with the classical arts of other times, or as he called it, to create an art like the Louvre out of impressionism. We shall find him striving always toward actualities, toward the realization of beauty as it is seen to exist in the real, in the object itself, whether it be mountain or apple or human, the entire series of living things in relation to one another.

It is consistent that Cézanne, like all pioneers, was without prescribed means, that he had to spend his life inventing for himself those terms and methods which would best express his feelings about nature. It is natural that he admired the precision of Bouguereau, it is also quite natural that he should have worshipped in turn, Delacroix, Courbet, and without doubt, the mastery of Ingres, and it is indicative too that he felt the frank force of Manet. It was his special distinction to strive toward a simple presentation of simple things, to want to paint "that which existed between himself and the object," and to strive to solidify the impressionistic conception with a greater realization of form in space, the which they had so much ignored. That he achieved this in a satisfying manner may be observed in the best of his landscapes and still-lifes, and in some of the figure studies also. The endeavor to eliminate all aspects of extraneous conception by dismissing the quality of literature, of poetry and romance from painting, was the exact characteristic which made him what he is for us today, the pioneer in the field of modern art. It was significant enough when he once said to Renoir, that it took him twenty years to find out that painting was not sculpture. Those earlier and heavy impasto studies of his are the evidence of this worthy deduction. It was significant, too, when he said that Gaugin was but "a flea on his back," and that "he does nothing but paint Chinese images."

The phrase that brings these two strikingly original personages in art together is the one of Cézanne: "I remain the primitive of the way I have discovered"; and that of Whitman, which comes if I am not mistaken from Democratic Vistas, though it may be from elsewhere in Whitman's prose, running chiefly: "I only wish to indicate the way for the innumerable poets that are to come after me," etc.,

and "I warn you this is not a book, this is a man."
These two geniuses are both of one piece as to their
esthetic intention, despite the great gulf that lies
between their concepts of, and their attitudes toward
life. For the one, life was a something to stay
close to always, for the other, it was something to
be afraid of to an almost abnormal degree; Whitman and his door never closed, Cézanne and his
door seldom or never opened, indeed, were heavily
padlocked against the intrusion of the imaginary
outsider. These are the geniuses who have done
most for these two arts of the present time, it is
Whitman and Cézanne who have clarified the sleeping eye and withheld it from being totally blinded,
from the onslaughts of jaded tradition.

There were in Cézanne the requisite gifts for
selection, and for discarding all useless encum-
brances, there was in him the great desire for purification, or of seeing the superb fact in terms of
itself, majestically; and if not always serenely,
serenity was nevertheless his passionate longing.
He saw what there was for him in those old and
accepted masters who meant most to him, and he
saw also what there was for him in that newest of
old masters, which was also in its way the assumed
discovery of our time, he saw the relativity of
Greco's beautiful art to the art of his own making.
He saw that here was a possible and applicable
architectonic suited to the objects of his newly conceived principles, he felt in Greco the magnetic

tendency of one thing toward another in nature, that trees and hills and valleys and people were not something sitting still for his special delectation, but that they were constantly aspiring to fruition, either physical, mental, or let us say, spiritual, even when the word is applied to the so-termed inanimate objects. He felt the "palpitancy," the breathing of all things, the urge outward of all life toward the light which helps it create and recreate itself. He felt this "movement" in and about things, and this it is that gives his pictures that sensitive life quality which lifts them beyond the aspect of picture-making or even mere representation. They are not cold studies of inanimate things, they are pulsing realizations of living substances striving toward each other, lending each other their individual activities until his canvases become, as one might name them, ensembles of animation, orchestrated life. We shall, I think, find this is what Greco did for Cézanne, and it is Cézanne who was among the first of moderns, if not the first, to appreciate that particular aspirational quality in the splendid pictures of Greco. They "move" toward their design, they were lifted by the quality of their organization into spaces in which they were free to carry on the fine illusion of life.

Whitman has certainly aspired equally, but being more things in one than Cézanne, his task has been in some ways greater, more difficult, and may we say for humanistic reasons, loftier. Whitman's inclusiveness was at one and the same time his virtue and his defect. For mystical reasons, it was imperative for him to include all things in himself, and so he set about enumerating all those elements which were in him, and of which he was so devoted and affectionate a part. That he could leave nothing out was, it may be said, his strongest esthetical defect, for it is by esthetical judgment that we choose and bring together those elements as we conceive it. It is the mark of good taste to reject that which is unessential, and the "tact of omission," well exemplified in Cézanne, has been found excellently axiomatic. So that it is the tendency in Whitman to catalogue in detail the entire obvious universe that makes many of his pages a strain on the mind as well as on the senses, and the eye especially. The absolute enforcement of this gift of omission in painting makes it easier for the artist, in that his mind is perforce engrossed with the idea of simplification, directness, and an easy relationship of the elements selected for presentation to each other.

It is the quality of "living-ness" in Cézanne that sends his art to the heights of universality, which is another way of naming the classical vision, or the masterly conception, and brings him together with Whitman as much of the same piece. You get all this in all the great masters of painting and literature, Goethe, Shakespeare, Rubens, and the Greeks. It is the reaching out and the very mastering of life which makes all art great, and all artists into geniuses. It is the specializing on ideas which shuts the stream of its flow. I have felt the same gift for life in a still-life or a landscape of Cézanne's that I have felt in any of Whitman's best pieces. The element in common with these two exceptional creators is liberation. They have done more, these modern pioneers, for the liberation of the artist, and for the "freeing" of painting and poetry than any other men of modern time. Through them, painting and poetry have become literally free, and through them it is that the young painters and poets have sought new fields for self deliverance Discipleship does not hold out long with the truly understanding. Those who really know what originality is are not long the slave of the power of imitation: it is the gifted assimilator that suffers most under the spell of mastery. Legitimate influence is a quality which all earnest creators learn to handle at once. Both poetry and painting are, or so it seems to me, revealing well the gift of understanding, and as a result we have a better variety of painting and of poetry than at the first outbreak of this so called modern esthetic epidemic.

The real younger creators are learning the difference between surface and depth, between exterior semblances, and the underlying substances. Both Whitman and Cézanne stand together in the name of one common purpose, freedom from characteristics not one's own. They have taught the creators of this time to know what classicism really is, that it is the outline of all things that endure. They have both shown that it is not idiosyncrasy alone which creates originality, that idiosyncrasy is but the husk of personal penetration, that it is in no way the constituent essential for genius. For genius is nothing but the name for higher perception, the greater degree of understanding. Cézanne's fine landscapes and still-lifes, and Whitman's majestic line with its gripping imagery are one and the same thing, for it reaches the same height in the mind. They walk together out of a vivid past, these two geniuses, opening the corridors to a possibly vivid future for the artists of now, and to come. They are the gateway for our modern esthetic development, the prophets of the new time. They are most of all, the primitives of the way they have begun, they have voiced most of all the imperative need of essential personalism, of direct expression out of direct experience, with an eye to nothing but quality and proportion as conceived by them. Their dogmas were both simple in the extreme, and of immense worth to us in their respective spheres. We may think of them as the giants of the beginning of the twentieth century, with the same burning desire to enlarge the general scope of vision, and the finer capacity for individual experience.

ALBERT P. RYDER

ALBERT P. RYDER possessed in a high degree that
strict passivity of mental vision which calls into being
the elusive yet fixed element the mystic Blake so
ardently refers to and makes a principle of, that
element outside the mind's jurisdiction. His work
is of the essence of poetry; it is alien to the realm
of esthetics pure, for it has very special spiritual his-
tories to relate. His landscapes are somewhat akin
to those of Michel and of Courbet. They suggest
Michel's wide wastes of prodigal sky and duneland
with their winding roads that have no end, his ever-
shadowy stretches of cloud upon ever-shadowy
stretches of land that go their austere way to the
edges of some vacant sea. They suggest, too, those
less remote but perhaps even more aloof spaces of
solitude which were ever Courbet's theme in his
deeper hours, that haunting sense of subtle habita-
tion, that acute invasion of either wind or soft fleck
of light or bright presence in a breadth of shadow,
as if a breath of living essences always somehow
pervaded those mystic woodland or still lowland
scenes. But highly populate as these pictures of
Courbet's are with the spirit of ever-passing feet
that hover and hold converse in the remote wood,
the remoter plain, they never quite surrender to that

ghostliness which possesses the pictures of our Ryder. At all times in his work one has the feeling of there having lately passed, if ever so fleetly, some bodily shape seeking a solitude of its own. I recall no other landscapes impressed with a more terrific austerity save Greco's incredible "Toledo," to my thinking a finality in landscape creation.

There is quietude, solace, if you will, in Michel, in Courbet, but there is never a rest for the eye or the mind or the spirit in those most awesome of pictures which Ryder has presented to us, few as they are; for the Ryder legend is akin to the legend of Giorgione. There is always splendor in them but it is the splendor of the dream given over to a genius more powerful than the vision which has conjured them forth. It is distinctly a land of Luthany in which they have their being; he has inscribed for us that utter homelessness of the spirit in the far tracts that exist in the realm of the imagination; there is suffering in his pictures, that fainting of the spirit, that breathlessness which overtakes the soul in search of the consummation of beauty.

Ryder is akin to Coleridge, too, for there is a direct visional analogy between "The Flying Dutchman" and the excessively pictorial stanzas of "The Ancient Mariner." Ryder has typified himself in this excellent portrayal of sea disaster, this profound spectacle of the soul's despair in conflict with wind and wave. Could any picture contain more of that remoteness of the world of our real heart as

ALBERT P. RYDER

well as our real eye, the artist's eye which visits that
world in no official sense but only as a guest or a
courtly spectator? No artist, I ought to say, was
ever more master of his ideas and less master of the
medium of painting than Ryder; there is in some of
his finest canvases a most pitiable display of ignorance which will undoubtedly shorten their life by
many years.

I still retain the vivid impression that afflicted me
when I saw my first Ryder, a marine of rarest gran-
deur and sublimity, incredibly small in size, incredibly large in its emotion—just a sky and a single
vessel in sail across a conquering sea. Ryder is,
I think, the special messenger of the sea's beauty,
the confidant of its majesties, its hauteurs, its su-
premacies; for he was born within range of the sea
and all its legends have hovered with him continually. Since that time I have seen a number of
other pictures either in the artist's possession or elsewhere: "Death on the Racetrack," "Pegasus," canvases from The Tempest and Macbeth in that
strange little world of chaos that was his home, his
hermitage, so distraught with débris of the world
for which he could seem to find no other place; I
have spent some of the rare and lovelier moments
of my experience with this gentlest and sweetest of
other-world citizens; I have felt with ever-living delight the excessive loveliness of his glance and of his
smile and heard that music of some far-away world
which was his laughter; I have known that wisdom

which is once and for all wisdom for the artist, that
confidence and trust that for the real artist there is
but one agency for the expression of self in terms
of beauty, the eye of the imagination, that mystical
third somewhere in the mind which transposes all
that is legitimate to expression. To Ryder the
imagination was the man; he was a poet painter,
living ever outside the realm of theory.

He was fond of Corot, and at moments I have
thought of him as the heir and successor to some of
Corot's haunting graces; but there was all the difference between them that there is between lyric
pure and tragic pure. Ryder has for once tran-
scribed all outer semblances by means of a personality unrelated to anything other than itself, an imagination belonging strictly to our soil and specifically
to our Eastern geography. In his autographic quality he is certainly our finest genius, the most creative, the most racial. For our genius, at its best,
is the genius of the evasive; we are born lovers of
the secret element, the mystery in things.

How many of our American painters have given
real attention to Ryder? I find him so much the
legend among professional artists, this master of
arabesque, this first and foremost of our designers,
this real creator of pattern, this first of all creators
of tragic landscape, whose pictures are sacred to
those that revere distinction and power in art. He
had in him that finer kind of reverence for the element of beauty which finds all things somehow

lovely. He understood best of all the meaning of the grandiose, of everything that is powerful; none of his associates in point of time rose to just that sublimated experience; not Fuller, not Martin, not Blakelock, though each of these was touched to a special expression. They are more derivative than Ryder, more the children of Barbizon.

Ryder gave us first and last an incomparable sense of pattern and austerity of mood. He saw with an all too pitiless and pitiful eye the element of helplessness in things, the complete succumbing of things in nature to those elements greater than they that wield a fatal power. Ryder was the last of the romantics, the last of that great school of impressive artistry, as he was the first of our real painters and the greatest in vision. He was a still companion of Blake in that realm of the beyond, the first citizen of the land of Luthany. He knew the fine distinction between drama and tragedy, the tragedy which nature prevails upon the sensitive to accept. He was the painter poet of the immanent in things.

WINSLOW HOMER

In Winslow Homer we have yankeeism of the first order, turned to a creditable artistic account. With a fierce feeling for truth, a mania, almost, for actualities, there must have been somewhere in his make-up a gentleness, a tenderness and refinement which explain his fine appreciation of the genius of the place he had in mind to represent. There is not an atom of legend in Homer, it is always and always narrative of the obvious world. There is at once the essential dramatic import ruling the scene. With him it is nothing but dramatic relationship, the actionary tendency of the facts themselves, in nature. You are held by him constantly to the bold and naked theme, and you are left to wander in the imagination only among the essentials of simple and common realism.

Narrative then, first and last with Homer, and the only creative aspect of his pictures is concealed in the technique. The only touch of invention in them is the desire to improve the language they speak. Dramatic always, I do not call them theatric excepting in the case of one picture that I know, called "Morro Castle" I think, now in the Metropolitan Museum, reminding me much of the commonplace, "Chateau de Chillon" of Courbet's,

42

neither of these pictures being of any value in the careers of their authors. But once you sat on the rocks of Maine, and watched the climbing of the surf up the morning sky after a heavy storm at sea, you realize the force of Homer's gift for the realities. His pictures are yankee in their indications, as a work of art could be, flinty and unyielding, resolute as is the yankee nature itself, or rather to say, the original yankee, which was pioneer then in a so rough yet resourceful country. It is the quality of Thoreau, but without the genius of Thoreau for the poetry of things.

Homer's pictures give you nothing but the bare fact told in the better class terms of illustration, for he was illustrator, first of all. While the others were trying to make a little American Barbizon of their own, there were Homer, Ryder, Fuller, Martin, working alone for such vastly opposite ideas, and yet, of these men, four of them were expressing such highly imaginative ideas, and Homer was the unflinching realist among them. I do not know where Homer started, but I believe it was the sea at Prout's Neck that taught him most. I think that William Morris Hunt and Washington Allston must have seemed like infant Michelangelos then, for there is still about them a sturdiness which we see little of in the American art of that time, or even now for that matter. They had a certain massive substance, proving the force of mind and personality which was theirs, and while these men were proving the abundance and warmth of themselves, Homer was the frozen one among them. Nature was nature to him, and that alone he realized, and yet it was not precisely slavish imitation that impelled him.

There was in him a very creditable sense of selection,—as will be seen especially in the water colours, so original with him, so gifted in their power of treatment—one of the few great masters of the medium the world has known. He knew the meaning of wash as few since have known it, he knew that it has scale and limitation of its own, and for all that, infinite suggestibility. Not Turner or Whistler have excelled him, and I do not know of anyone who has equalled him in understanding of this medium outside of Dodge Macknight and John Marin. It is in these so expressive paintings on paper that you feel the real esthetic longing as well as a certain contribution in Homer, the desire to realize himself and to release himself from too slavish imitation of nature and the too rigid consideration of truth. He was finer in technique than perhaps any that I have mentioned, though the two modern men have seconded him very closely, and in point of vision have, I am certain, surpassed him. Homer arrived because of his power to express what he wished to say, though his reach was far less lofty than theirs. He was essentially on the ground, and wanted to paint the very grip of his own feet on the rocks. He wanted the inevitability put down in

recognizable form. He had not feeling for the hint
or the suggestion until he came to the water-color,
which is of course most essentially that sort of medium. He knew its scope and its limitations and
never stepped out of its boundaries, and he achieved
a fine mastery in it. His imitators will never arrive at his severity because they are not flint yankee. They have not the hard head and snappy
tongue. It was yankee crabbedness that gave
Homer his grip on the idea he had in mind. Florida lent a softer tone to what Maine rocks could
not give him. He is American from skin to skeleton, and a leader among yankee as well as American geniuses. He probably hated as much as
Thoreau, and in his steely way admired as much.
It was fire from the flintlock in them both, though
nature had a far softer and loftier persuasion with
the Concord philosopher and naturalist.

Homer remains a figure in our American culture
through his feeling for reality. He has learned
through slavery to detail to put down the essential
fact, however abundantly or however sparsely. He
has a little of Courbet's sense of the real, and none
whatever of his sense of the imaginative. It was
enough for him to classicize the realistic incident.
He impels me to praise through his yankee insistence upon integrity. Story is story with Homer and
he leaves legend to itself. It is the narrative of
the Whittier type, homely, genuine, and typical.
He never stepped outside of his yankee determina-

tion.   Homer has sent the art of water colour painting to a very high place in world consideration.
He cannot be ignored as a master in this field.   His
paintings must be taken as they are, solid renderings
of fact, dramatically considered.   He offers nothing else.   Once you have seen these realistic sea
pictures, you may want to remember and you may
want to forget, but they call for consideration.
They are true in their living appreciation of reality.

He knew the sea like the old salts that were his
neighbors, and from accounts he was as full of the
tang of the sea as they.   He was a foe to compromise and a despiser of imposition.   The best and
most impersonal of him is in his work, for he never
ventured to express philosophies, ethics, or morals
in terms of picture-painting.   That is to his credit
at least.   He was concerned with illustration first
and last, as he was illustrator and nothing else.
He taught the proceeding school of illustrators
much in the significance of verity, and in the ways
and means of expressing verity in terms of pigment.
What the stiff pen and ink drawings and the cold
engravings of his time taught him, he conferred
upon the later men in terms of freedom of technique.   And at the same time he rose a place, as
painter and artist of no mean order, by a certain
distinction inherent in him.   He had little feeling
for synthesis outside of the water-colours, and here
it was necessary by virtue of the limitations of the
medium.

WINSLOW HOMER

Winslow Homer will not stimulate for all time only because his mind was too local. There is nothing of universal appeal in him. His realism will never reach the height even of the sea-pieces of Courbet, and I shall include Ryder as well. Courbet was a fine artist, and so was Ryder, and both had the advantage of exceptional imagination. Homer and Ryder are natives of the same coast and typify excellently the two poles in the New England temper, both in art and in life. Homer as realist, had the one idea in mind only, to illustrate realism as best he could in the most distinguished terms at the disposal of his personality. He succeeded admirably.

Homer typifies a certain sturdiness in the American temper at least, and sends the lighter men away with his roughness, as doubtless he sent the curious away from his cliffs with the acidity of truth he poured upon them. He had lived so much in the close association of the roughest elements in existence, rocks and the madly swinging sea that glides over and above them defiantly, that he had without doubt taken on the character of them. The portrait of Homer gives him as one would expect him to look, and he looks like his pictures. His visage bore a ferocity that had to be met with a rocky certainty. It is evident there was no fooling him. He was filled with yankee tenacity and yankee courage. Homer is what you would expect to find if you were told to hunt up the natives of "Prout's Neck" or

"Perkins Cove," or any of the inlets of the Maine coast. These sea people live so much with the roughness of the sea, that if they are at all inclined to acidity, and the old fashioned yankee was sure to be, they take on the hard edges of a man's temper in accordance with the jaggedness of the shores on which they live. The man around the rocks looks so very like the profiles one sees in the rocks themselves. They have absorbed the energy of the dramatic elements they cope with, and you may be sure that life around the sea in New England is no easy existence; and they give out the same salty equivalent in human association.

If you have lived by the sea, you have learned the significance of the bravery of sea people, and you learn to understand and excuse the sharpness of them which is given them from battle with the elemental facts they are confronted with at all times. That is the character of Homer, that is the quality of his painting. That is what makes him original in the American sense, and so recognizable in the New England sense. He is one of New England's strongest spokesmen, and takes his place by the side of Ryder, Thoreau, Hawthorne, Fuller, Whittier, and such representative temperaments, and it is this quality that distinguishes him from men like Inness, Wyant, and the less typical painters. It is obvious, too, that he never painted any other coast, excepting of course Florida, in the water colours.

WINSLOW HOMER

It was Florida that produced the chef d'œuvre in him. It was Maine that taught him the force of the southern aspect. Romancer among the realistic facts of nature, he might be called, for he did not merely copy nature. He did invest things with their own suggestive reality, and he surmounted his earlier gifts for exact illustration by this other finer gift for romantic appreciation. Homer was an excellent narrator, as will be seen in the "Gulf Stream" picture in the Metropolitan Museum. It has the powers of Jack London and of Conrad in it. Homer was intense, vigorous, and masculine. If he was harsh in his characteristics, he was one who knew the worth of economy in emotion. He was one with his idea and his metier, and that is sufficient.

AMERICAN VALUES IN PAINTING

THERE are certain painters who join themselves together in a kind of grouping, which, whether they wish to think of themselves in this light or not, have become in the matter of American values in painting, a fixed associative aspect of painting in America. When we speak of American painting, the choice is small, but definite as to the number of artists, and the type of art they wished themselves to be considered for. From the Hudson River grouping, which up to Inness is not more marked than as a set of men copying nature with scrupulous fidelity to detail, rather than conveying any special feeling or notion of what a picture of, or the landscape itself, may convey; and leaving aside the American pupils of the Academy in Paris and Rome, most of whom returned with a rich sense of rhetorical conventionalities in art—men like William Morris Hunt and Washington Allston—we may turn to that other group of men as being far more typical of our soil and temper. I mean artists such as Homer Martin, Albert P. Ryder, George Fuller, and the later Winslow Homer who certainly did receive more recognition than any of them prior to his death.

Martin, Ryder, and Fuller could not have enjoyed much in the way of appreciation outside of a few artists of their time, and even now they may be said to be the artists for artists. It is reasonable to hope that they were not successful, since that which was à la mode in the expression of their time was essentially of the dry Academy. One would hardly think of Homer Martin's "Border of the Seine" landscape in the Metropolitan Museum, hardly more then than now, and it leaves many a painter flat in appreciation of its great dignity, austerity, reserve, and for the distinguished quality of its stylism. What Martin may have gotten, during his stay in Europe, which is called impressionism is, it must be said, a more aristocratic type of impressionism than issued from the Monet followers. Martin must then have been knowing something of the more dignified intellectualism of Pissarro and of Sisley, those men who have been the last to reach the degrees of appreciation due them in the proper exactitude.

We cannot think of Martin as ever having carried off academic medals during his period. We cannot think of Martin as President of the Academy, which position was occupied by a far inferior artist who was likewise carried away by impressionism, namely Alden Weir. The actual attachment in characteristic of introspective temper in Alden Weir is not so removed from Martin, Fuller and Ryder as might be imagined; he is more like Martin perhaps though far less profound in his sense of mystery; Fuller being more the romanticist and Ryder in my estimation the greatest romanticist, and artist as well, of all of these men. But Alden Weir failed to carry off any honor as to distinctive qualities and invention. A genial aristocrat if you will, but having for me no marked power outside of a Barbizonian interest in nature with a kind of mystical detachedness.

But in the consideration of painters like Martin, Fuller and Ryder we are thinking chiefly of their relation to their time as well as their relation to what is to come in America. America has had as much painting considering its youth as could be expected of it and the best of it has been essentially native and indigenous. But in and out of the various influences and traditional tendencies, these several artists with fine imaginations, typical American imaginations, were proceeding with their own peculiarly original and significantly personal expressions. They represent up to their arrival, and long after as well, all there is of real originality in American painting, and they remain for all time as fine examples of artists with purely native imaginations, working out at great cost their own private salvations for public discovery at a later time.

All these men were poor men with highly distinguished aristocratic natures and powerful physiques, as to appearances, with mentalities much beyond the average. When an exhibition of modern American painting is given, as it surely will and must be, these men and not the Barbizonian echoes as represented by Inness, Wyant & Co., will represent for us the really great beginning of art in America. There will follow naturally artists like Twachtman and Robinson, as likewise Kenneth Hayes Miller and Arthur B. Davies for reasons that I think are rather obvious: both Hayes Miller and Arthur B. Davies having skipped over the direct influence of impressionism by reason of their attachment to Renaissance ideas; having joined themselves by conviction in perhaps slight degrees to aspects of modern painting.   Miller is, one might say, too intellectually deliberate to allow for spontaneities which mere enthusiasms encourage.   Miller is emotionally thrilled by Renoir but he is never quite swept.   His essential conservatism hinders such violence.   It would be happier for him possibly if the leaning were still more pronounced.

The jump to modernism in Arthur B. Davies results in the same sort of way as admixture of influence though it is more directly appreciable in him. Davies is more willing, by reason of his elastic temper and intellectual vivacity, to stray into the field of new ideas with a simple though firm belief, that they are good while they last, no matter how long they last.   Davies is almost a propagandist in his feeling for and admiration of the ultra-modern movement.   Miller is a questioner and ponders long upon every point of consequence or inconsequence.   He is a metaphysical analyst which is perhaps the extraneous element in his painting.   In his etching, that is, the newest of it, one feels the sense of the classical and the modern joined together and by the classical I mean the quality of Ingres, conjoined with modern as in Renoir, relieved of the influence of Italian Renaissance.

But I do not wish to lose sight of these several forerunners in American art, Martin, Ryder and Fuller who, in their painting, may be linked not without relativity to our artists in literary imagination, Hawthorne and Poe. Fuller is conspicuously like Hawthorne, not by his appreciation of witchcraft merely, but by his feeling for those eery presences which determine the fates of men and women in their time. Martin is the purer artist for me since he seldom or never resorted to the literary emotion in the sense of drama or narrative, whereas in the instances of Ryder or Fuller they built up expression entirely from literary experience. Albert Ryder achieves most by reason of his vaster poetic sensibility—his Homeric instincts for the drama and by a very original power for arabesque. He is alone among the Americans in his unique gift for pattern. We can claim Albert Ryder as our most original painter as Poe takes his place as our most original poet who had of course one of the greatest and most perfect imaginations of his time and possibly of all time.

But it is these several painters I speak of, Martin, Ryder, and Fuller, who figure for us as the originators of American indigenous painting. They will not be copied for they further nothing beyond themselves. No influence of these painters has been notable, excepting for a time in the early experience of one of the younger modernists who, by reason of definite associations of birthright and relativity of environment, essayed to claim Albert Ryder as a very definite influence; just as Courbet and Corot must in their ways have been powerful influences upon Ryder himself. Albert Ryder is too much of a figure to dismiss here with group-relationship, he must be treated of separately. So far then, there is no marked evidence that the influence of Fuller or Martin was powerful enough to carry beyond themselves. They had no tenets or theories other than those of personal clarification. All three remained the hermit radicals of life, as they remain isolated examples in American art; and all of them essentially of New England, in that they were conspicuously introspective, and shut in upon their own exclusive experience.

But for all these variances, we shall find Homer Martin, George Fuller, and Albert Ryder forming the first nucleus for a definite value in strictly American painting. They were conscious of nothing really outside of native associations and native deductions. The temper of them is as essentially American as the quality of them is essentially Eastern in flavor. They seldom ventured beyond more than a home-spun richness of color, though in

Ryder's case Monticelli had assisted very definitely in his notion of the volume of tone. We find here then despite the impress of artists like William Morris Hunt, Washington Allston, and the later Inness with the still later Winslow Homer, that gripping and relentless realist who took hold of the newer school of painter-illustrators, that the artists treated of here may be considered as the most important phase of American painting in the larger sense of the term. If I were to assist in the arrangement of an all American exhibition to show the trend toward individualism I should begin with Martin, Fuller and Ryder. I should then proceed to Winslow Homer, John H. Twachtman, Theodore Robinson, Hayes Miller, Arthur B. Davies, Rockwell Kent, then to those who come under the eighteen-ninety tendency in painting, namely the Whistler-Goya-Velasquez influence.

From this it will be found that an entirely new development had taken place among a fairly large group of younger men who came, and very earnestly, under the Cézannesque influence. It may be said that the choice of these men is a wise one for it is conspicuous among artists of today that since Cézanne art will never, cannot ever be the same, just as with Delacroix and Courbet a French art could never have remained the same. Impressionism will be found to have had a far greater value as a suggestive influence than as a creative one. It brought light in as a scientific aspect into modern painting and that is its valuable contribution. So it is that with Cézanne the world is conscious of a new power that will never be effectually shaken off, since the principles that are involved in the intention of Cézanne are of too vital importance to be treated with lightness of judgment. Such valuable ideas as Cézanne contributes must be accepted almost as dogma, albeit valuable dogma. Influence is a conscious and necessary factor in the development of all serious minded artists, as we have seen in the instances of all important ones.

So it is I feel that the real art of America, and it can, I think, justly be said that there is such, will be headed by the imaginative artists I have named in point of their value as indigenous creators, having worked out their artistic destinies on home soil with all the virility of creators in the finer sense of the term. They have assisted in the establishment of a native tradition which without question has by this time a definite foundation. The public must be made aware of their contribution to a native production. It will no doubt be a matter for surprise to many people in the world today that art in general is more national or local than it has ever been, due mostly to the recent upheaval, which has been of great service to the re-establishment of art interest and art appreciation everywhere in the modern world. Art, like life, has had to begin all over again, for the very end of the world had been made visible at last. The artist may look safely over an utterly new horizon, which is the only encouragement the artist of today can hope for.

MODERN ART IN AMERICA

THE question may be asked, what is the hope of modern art in America? The first reply would be that modern art will one day be realized in America if only from experience we learn that all things happen in America by means of the epidemical principle. It is of little visible use that single individuals, by sitting in the solitary confinement of their as yet little understood enthusiasms, shall hope to achieve what is necessary for the American idea, precisely as necessary for us here as for the peoples of Europe who have long since recognized that any movement toward expression is a movement of unquestionable importance. Until the moment when public sincerity and the public passion for excitement is stimulated, the vague art interests of America will go on in their dry and conventional manner. The very acute discernment of Maurice Vlaminck that "intelligence is international, stupidity is national, art is local" is a valuable deduction to make, and applies in the two latter instances as admirably to America as to any other country. Our national stupidity in matters of esthetic modernity is a matter for obvious acceptance, and not at all for amazement.

That art is local is likewise just as true of America as of any other country, and despite the judgment of stodgy minds, there is a definite product which is peculiar to our specific temper and localized sensibility as it is of any other country which is nameable. Despite the fact that impressionism is still exaggeration, and that large sums are still being paid for a "sheep-piece" of Charles Jacque, as likewise for a Ridgeway Knight, there is a well defined grouping of younger painters working for a definitely localized idea of modernism, just as in modern poetry there is a grouping of poets in America who are adding new values to the English language, as well as assisting in the realization of a freshly evolved localized personality in modern poetics.

Art in America is like a patent medicine, or a vacuum cleaner. It can hope for no success until ninety million people know what it is. The spread of art as "culture" in America is from all appearances having little or no success because stupidity in such matters is so national. There is a very vague consideration of modern art among the directors of museums and among art dealers, but the comprehension is as vague as the interest. Outside of a Van Gogh exhibition, a few Matisses, now and then a Cézanne exhibited with great feeling of condescension, there is little to show the American public that art is as much a necessity as a substantial array of food is to an empty stomach. The public hunger cannot groan for what it does not recognize as real nourishment. There is no reason in the world why America does not have as many chances to see modern art as Europe has, save for minor matters of distance. The peoples of the world are alike, sensibilities are of the same nature everywhere among the so-called civilized, and it must be remembered always that the so-called primitive races invented for their own racial salvation what was not to be found ready made for them. Modern art is just as much of a necessity to us as art was to the Egyptians, the Assyrians, the Greeks. Those peoples have the advantage of us only because they were in a higher state of culture as a racial unit. They have no more of a monopoly upon the idea of rhythm and organization than we have, because that which was typical of the human consciousness then, is typical of it now. As a result of the war, there has been, it must be said, a heightening of national consciousness in all countries, because creative minds that were allowed to survive were sent home to struggle with the problem of their own soil.

There is no reason whatever for believing that America cannot have as many good artists as any other country. It simply does not have them because the integrity of the artist is trifled with by the intriguing agencies of materialism. Painters find the struggle too keen and it is easy to become the advertising designer, or the merchant in painting, which is what many of our respectable artists have become. The lust for prosperity takes the place of artistic integrity and courage. But America need not be surprised to find that it has a creditable grouping of artists sufficiently interested in the value of modern art as an expression of our time, men and possibly some women, who feel that art is a matter of private aristocratic satisfaction at least, until the public is awakened to the idea that art is an essentially local affair and the more local it becomes by means of comprehension of the international character, the truer it will be to the place in which it is produced.

A catalogue of names will suffice to indicate the character and variation of the localized degree of expression we are free to call American in type: Morgan Russell, S. Macdonald Wright, Arthur G. Dove, William Yarrow, Dickinson, Thomas H. Benton, Abraham Walkowitz, Max Weber, Ben Benn, John Marin, Charles Demuth, Charles Sheeler, Marsden Hartley, Andrew Dasburg, William McFee, Man Ray, Walt Kuhn, John Covert, Morton Schamberg, Georgia O'Keeffe, Stuart Davis, Rex Slinkard. Added to these, the three modern photographers Alfred Stieglitz, Charles Sheeler, and Paul Strand must be included. Besides these indigenous names, shall we place the foreign artists whose work falls into line in the movement toward modern art in America, Joseph Stella, Marcel Duchamp, Gaston Lachaise, Eli Nadelman. There may be no least questioning as to how much success all of these artists would have in their respective ways in the various groupings that prevail in Europe at this time. They would be recognized at once for the authenticity of their experience and for their integrity as artists gifted with international intelligence. There is no reason to feel that prevailing organizations like the Society of Independent Artists, Inc., and the Société Anonyme, Inc., will not bear a great increase of influence and power upon the public, as there is every reason to believe that at one time or another the public will realize what is being done for them by these societies, as well as what was done by the so famous "291" gallery.

The effect however is not vast enough because the public finds no shock in the idea of art. It is not melodramatic enough and America must be appealed to through its essentially typical melodramatic instincts. There is always enough music, and there are some who certainly can say altogether too much of the kind there is in this country. The same thing can be said of painting. There is altogether too much of comfortable art, the art of the uplifted illustration. It is the reflex of the Anglo-Saxon passion for story-telling in pictures which should be relegated to the field of the magazines. Great art often tells a story but great art is always something plus the idea. Ordinary art does not rise above it.

I often wonder why it is that America, which is essentially a country of sports and gamblers, has not the European courage as well as rapacity for fresh development in cultural matters. Can it be because America is not really intelligent? I should

63

be embarrassed in thinking so. There is nevertheless an obvious lethargy in the appreciation of creative taste and a still lingering yet old-fashioned faith in the continual necessity for importation. America has a great body of assimilators, and out of this gift for uncreative assimilation has come the type of art we are supposed to accept as our own. It is not at all difficult to prove that America has now an encouraging and competent group of young and vigorous synthesists who are showing with intelligence what they have learned from the newest and most engaging development of art, which is to say—modern art. The names which have been inserted above are the definite indication, and one may go so far as to say proof, of this argument that modern art in America is rapidly becoming an intelligently localized realization.

OUR IMAGINATIVES

Is it vision that creates temperament or temperament that creates vision? Physical vision is responsible for nearly everything in art, not the power to see but the way to see. It is the eye perfect or the eye defective that determines the kind of thing seen and how one sees it. It was certainly a factor in the life of Lafcadio Hearn, for he was once named the poet of myopia. It was the acutely sensitive eye of Cézanne that taught him to register so ably the minor and major variations of his theme. Manet saw certainly far less colour than Renoir, for in the Renoir sense he was not a colourist at all. He himself said he painted only what he saw. Sight was almost science with Cézanne as it was passion.

In artists like Homer Martin there is a something less than visual accuracy and something more than a gift of translation. There is a distinguished interpretation of mood coupled with an almost miniature-like sense of delicate gradation, and at the same time a something lacking as to a sense of physical form. In the few specimens of Martin to be seen there is, nevertheless, eminent distinction paramount. He was an artist of "oblique integrity": He saw unquestionably at an angle, but the angle was a beau-

65

tiful one, and while many of his associates were doing American Barbizon, he was giving forth a shy, yet rare kind of expression, always a little symbolic in tendency, with the mood far more predominant. In "The sand dunes of Ontario" there will be found at once a highly individualistic feeling for the waste places of the world. There is never so much as a hint of banality in his selection. He never resorts to stock rhetoric.

Martin will be remembered for his singularly personal touch along with men like Fuller and Ryder. He is not as dramatic as either of these artists, but he has greater finesse in delicate sensibility. He was, I think, actually afraid of repetition, a characteristic very much in vogue in his time, either conscious or unconscious, in artists like Inness, Wyant, and Blakelock, with their so single note. There is exceptional mysticity hovering over his hills and stretches of dune and sky. It is not fog, or rain, or dew enveloping them. It is a certain veiled presence in nature that he sees and brings forward. His picture of peaks of the White Mountains, Jefferson and Madison, gives you no suggestion of the "Hudson River" emptiness. He was searching for profounder realities. He wanted the personality of his places, and he was successful, for all of his pictures I have seen display the magnetic touch. He "touched it off" vividly in all of them. They reveal their ideas poetically and esthetically and the method is personal and ample for presentation.

OUR IMAGINATIVES

With George Fuller it was vastly different. He seemed always to be halting in the shadow. You are conscious of a deep and ever so earnest nature in his pictures. He impressed himself on his canvases in spite of his so faulty expression. He had an understanding of depth but surface was strange to him. He garbled his sentences so to speak with excessive and useless wording. "The Octoroon" shows a fine feeling for romance as do all of the other pictures of Fuller that have been publicly visible, but it is romance obsessed with monotone. There is the evidence of extreme reticence and moodiness in Fuller always. I know little of him save that I believe he experienced a severity of domestic problems. Farmer I think he was, and painted at off hours all his life. It is the poetry of a quiet, almost sombre order, walking in the shadow on the edge of a wood being almost too much of an appearance for him in the light of a busy world.

Why is it I think of Hawthorne when I think of Fuller? Is there a relationship here, or is it only a similarity of eeriness in temper? I would suspect Fuller of having painted a Hester Prynne excepting that he could never have come to so much red in one place in his pictures.

There was vigour in these strong, simple men, masculine in sensibility all of them, and a fine feeling for the poetic shades of existence. They were intensely serious men, and I think from their isolation in various ways, not popular in their time. Neither are they popular now. They will only be admired by artists of perception, and by laymen of keen sensibility. Whether their enforced isolations taught them to brood, or whether they were brooders by nature, it is difficult to say. I think they were all easterners, and this would explain away certain characteristic shynesses of temper and of expression in them. Ryder, as we know, was the typical recluse, Fuller in all likelihood also. Martin I know little of privately, but his portrait shows him to be a strong elemental nature, with little feeling for, or interest in, the superficialities either of life or of art. Of Blakelock I can say but little, for I do not know him beyond a few stylish canvases which seem to have more of Diaz and Rousseau in them than contributes to real originality, and he was one of the painters of repetition also. A single good Blakelock is beautiful, and I think he must be included among the American imaginatives, but I do not personally feel the force of him in several canvases together.

All of these artists are singularly individual, dreamers like Mathew Maris and Marées of Europe. They all have something of Coleridge about them, something of Poe, something of the "Ancient Mariner" and the "Haunted Palace", sailors in the same ship, sleepers in the same house. All of these men were struggling at the same time, the painters I mean, the same hour it might be said,

OUR IMAGINATIVES

in the midst of conventions of a severer type of rigidity than now, to preserve themselves from commonplace utterance. They were not affected by fashions. They had the one idea in mind, to express themselves in terms of themselves, and they were singularly successful in this despite the various difficulties of circumstance and of temper that attended them. They understood what this was better than anyone, and the results in varying degrees of genius attest to the quality of the American imagination at its best.

I should like, for purposes of reference, to see a worthy exhibition of all of these men in one place. It would I am sure prove my statement that the eastern genius is naturally a tragic one, for all of these men have hardly once ventured into the clear sunlight of the world of every day. It would offset highly also, the superficial attitude that there is no imagination in American painting. We should not find so much of form or of colour in them in the stricter meaning of these ideas, as of mood. They might have set themselves to be disciples of William Blake's significant preachment, "put off intellect and put on imagination, the imagination is the man"; the intellect being the cultivated man, and the imagination being the natural man. There is imagination which by reason of its power and brilliance exceeds all intellectual effort, and effort at intellectualism is worse than a fine ignorance by far. Men who are highly imaginative, create by feeling what they do

69

not or cannot know. It is the sixth sense of the creator.

These artists were men alone, touched with the pristine significance of nature. It was pioneering of a difficult nature, precarious as all individual investigation of a spiritual or esthetic character is sure to be. Its first requisite is isolation, its last requisite is appreciation. All of these painters are gone over into that place they were so eager to investigate, illusion or reality. Their pictures are witness here to their seriousness. They testify to the bright everlastingness of beauty. If they have not swayed the world, they have left a dignified record in the art of a given time. Their contemporary value is at least inestimable. They are among the very first in the development of esthetics in America in point of merit. They made no compromise, and their record is clear.

If one looks over the record of American art up to the period of ultra-modernism, it will be found that these men are the true originals among American painters. We shall find outside of them and a very few others, so much of sameness, a certain academic convention which, however pronounced or meagre the personalities are, leave those personalities in the category of "safe" painters. They do not disturb by an excessively intimate point of view toward art or toward nature. They come up to gallery requirements by their "pleasantness" or the inoffensiveness of their style. They offer little in the way of interpretive power or synthetic understanding. It is the tendency to keep on the comfortable side in American art. Doubtless it is more practical as any innovator or investigator has learned for himself. Artists like Ryder and Martin and Fuller had nothing in common with market appreciations. They had ideas to express, and were sincere to the last in expressing them.

You will find little trace of commercialism in these men, even when, as in the case of Martin and Ryder and I do not know whom else, they did panels for somebody-or-other's leather screen, of which "Smuggler's Cove" and the other long panel of Ryder's in the Metropolitan Museum are doubtless two. They were not successful in their time because they could not repeat their performances. We know the efforts that were once made to make Ryder comfortable in a conventional studio, which he is supposed to have looked into once; and then he disappeared, as it was altogether foreign to him. Each picture was a new event in the lives of these men, and had to be pondered over devoutly, and for long periods often, as in the case of Ryder. Work was for him nine-tenths reflection and meditation and poetic brooding, and he put down his sensations on canvas with great difficulty in the manner of a labourer. It seems obvious that his first drafts were always vivid with the life intended for them, but no one could possibly have suffered with the idea of how to complete a picture more than he. His lack of facility held him from spontaneity, as it is likewise somewhat evident in Martin, and still more in Fuller.

They were artists in timidity, and had not the courage of physical force in painting. With them it was wholly a mental process. But we shall count them great for their purity of vision as well as for the sincerity and conviction that possessed them. Artistry of this sort will be welcomed anywhere, if only that we may take men seriously who profess seriousness. There is nothing really antiquated about sincerity, though I think conventional painters are not sure of that. It is not easy to think that men consent to repeat themselves from choice, and yet the passing exhibitions are proof of that. Martin and Ryder and Fuller refresh us with a poetic and artistic validity which places them out of association among men of their time or of today, in the field of objective and illustrative painters. We turn to them with pleasure after a journey through the museums, for their reticence let us say, and for the refinement of their vision, their beautiful gift of restraint. They emphasize the commonness of much that surrounds them, much that blatantly would obscure them if they were not pronouncedly superior. They would not be discounted to any considerable degree if they were placed among the known masters of landscape painters of all modern time. They would hold their own by the verity of feeling that is in them, and what they might lose in technical excellence, would be com-

OUR IMAGINATIVES

pensated for in uniqueness of personality. I should
like well to see them placed beside artists like Maris
and Marées, and even Courbet. It would surprise
the casual appreciator much, I believe.

73

OUR IMPRESSIONISTS

I HAVE for purely personal reasons chosen the two painters who formulate for me the conviction that there have been and are but two consistently convincing American impressionists. These gentlemen are John H. Twachtman and Theodore Robinson. I cannot say precisely in what year Twachtman died but for purposes intended here this data is of no paramount consequence, save that it is always a matter of query as to just how long an artist must live, or have been dead, to be discovered in what is really his own time.

John H. Twachtman as artist is difficult to know even by artists; for his work is made difficult to see either by its scarcity as determined for himself or by the exclusiveness of the owners of his pictures. It requires, however, but two or three of them to convince one that Twachtman has a something "plus" to contribute to his excursions into impressionism. One feels that after a Duesseldorf blackness which permeates his earlier work his conversion to impressionism was as fortunate as it was sincere. Twachtman knew, as is evidenced everywhere in his work, what he wished to essay and he proceeded with poetic reticence to give it forth. With a lyricism that is as convincing as it is authentic, you feel that

74

there is a certain underlying spirit of resignation. He surely knew that a love of sunlight would save any man from pondering on the inflated importance of world issues.

Having seen Twachtman but once my memory of his face recalls this admixture of emotion. He cared too much for the essential beauties to involve them with analyses extraneous to the meaning of beauty. That the Japanese did more for him than any other Orientals of whom he might have been thinking, is evident. For all that, his own personal lyricism surmounts his interest in outer interpretations of light and movement, and he leaves you with his own notion of a private and distinguished appreciation of nature. In this sense he leads one to Renoir's way of considering nature which was the pleasure in nature for itself. It was all too fine an adventure to quibble about.

Twachtman's natural reticence and, I could also believe, natural skepticism kept him from swinging wildly over to the then new theories, a gesture typical of less intelligent natures. He had the good sense to feel out for himself just where the new theories related to himself and set about producing flat simplicity of planes of color to produce a very distinguished notion of light. He dispensed with the photographic attitude toward objectivity and yet at the same time held to the pleasing rhythmical shapes in nature. He did not resort to divisionalism or to ultra-violence of relationship. The pictures that I have seen such as "February", for instance, in the Boston Museum, present for me the sensation of a man of great private spiritual and intellectual means, having the wish to express tactfully and convincingly his personal conclusions and reactions, leaning always toward the side of iridescent illusiveness rather than emotional blatancy and irrelevant extravagance. His nuances are perhaps too finely adjusted to give forth the sense of overwhelming magic either in intention or of execution. It is lyrical idea with Twachtman with seldom or never a dramatic gesture. He is as illusive as a phrase of Mallarmé and it will be remembered that he is of the period more or less of the rose and the lily and the lost idea in poetry. He does recall in essence at least the quality of pastels in prose, though the art intention is a sturdier one. It is enough that Twachtman did find his relationship to impressionism, and that he did not evolve a system of repetition which marks the failure of all influence.

Twachtman remains an artist of super-fine sensibility and distinction, and whatever he may have poured into the ears of students as an instructor left no visible haggard traces on his own production other than perhaps limiting that production. But we know that while the quality is valuable in respect of power it has no other precise value. We remember that Giorgione perished likewise with an uncertain product to his credit, as to numbers, but he did leave his immemorial impression. So it is with John

OUR IMPRESSIONISTS

H. Twachtman. He leaves his indelible influence among Americans as a fine artist, and he may be said to be among the few artists who, having taken up the impressionistic principle, found a way to express his personal ideas with a true degree of personal force. He is a beautifully sincere product and that is going far. Those pictures I have seen contain no taint of the market or clamoring for praise even. They were done because their author had an unobtrusive yet very aristocratic word to say, and the word was spoken with authority. John H. Twachtman must be counted as one of the genuine American artists, as well as among the most genuine artists of the world. If his pictures do not torment one with problematic intellectualism, they do hold one with their inherent refinement of taste and a degree of aristocratic approach which his true intelligence implies.

With the work of Theodore Robinson, there comes a wide divergence of feeling that is perhaps a greater comprehension of the principles of impressionism as applied to the realities involved in the academic principle. One is reminded of Bastien Le Page and Léon L'Hermitte, in the paintings of Robinson, as to their type of subject and the conception of them also. That he lived not far from Giverney is likewise evident. Being of New England yankee extraction, a Vermonter I believe, he must have essayed always a sense of economy in emotion. No one could have gone so far as the then incredible Monet, whose pictures wear us to indifference with vapid and unprofitable thinking. What Monet did was to encourage a new type of audacity and a brand-new type in truth, when no one had up to then attempted to see nature as prismatical under the direct influence of the solar rays. All this has since been worked out with greater exactitude by the later theorists in modernism.

While Van Gogh was slowly perishing of a mad ecstasy for light, covering up a natural Dutch realism with fierce attempts at prismatic relationship, always with the rhythms in a state of ecstatic ascendency; and Seurat had come upon the more satisfying pointillism as developed by himself; somewhere in amid all these extravagances men like Robinson were trying to combine orthodoxy of heritage and radicalist conversion with the new and very noble idea of impressionism. That Robinson succeeded in a not startling but nevertheless honorable and respectable fashion, must be conceded him. I sometimes think that Vignon, a seemingly obscure associate of the impressionists, with a similar impassioned feeling of realism, outdid him and approached closer to the principles as understood by Pissarro: probably better by a great deal than Monet himself, who is accredited with the honor of setting the theme moving in a modern line of that day. And Pissarro must have been a man to have so impressed all the men young and old of his time. After seeing a great number of Monet's one turns to any simple Pissarro for relief. And then there was also Sisley.

OUR IMPRESSIONISTS

But the talk is of Theodore Robinson. He holds his place as a realist with hardly more than a realist's conception, subjoined to a really pleasing appreciation of the principles of impressionism as imbibed by him from the source direct. Here are, then, the two true American impressionists, who, as far as I am aware, never slipped into the banalities of reiteration and marketable self-copy. They seem to have far more interest in private intellectual success than in a practical public one. It is this which helped them both, as it helps all serious artists, to keep their ideas clean of outward taint. This is one of the most important factors, which gives a man a place in the art he essays to achieve. When the day of his work is at an end it will be seen by everyone precisely what the influences were that prompted his effort toward deliverance through creation. It is for the sake of this alone that sincere artists keep to certain principles, and with genuine sacrifice often, as was certainly the case with Twachtman. And after all, how can a real artist be concerned as to just how salable his product is to be? Certainly not while he is working, if he be decent toward himself.. This is of course heresy, with Wall Street so near.

79

ARTHUR B. DAVIES

IF Arthur B. Davies had found it necessary, as in the modern time it has been found necessary to separate literature from painting, we should doubtless have had a very delicate and sensitive lyric poetry in book form. Titles for pictures like "Mirrored Dreaming," "Sicily-Flowering Isle," "Shell of Gold," "A Portal of the Night," "Mystic Dalliance," are all of them creations of an essentially poetic and literary mind. They are all splendid titles for a real book of legendary experience. The poet will be first to feel the accuracy of lyrical emotion in these titles. The paintings lead one away entirely into the land of legend, into the iridescent splendor of reflection. They take one out of a world of didactic monotone, as to their artistic significance. They are essentially pictures created for the purpose of transportation.

From the earlier days in that underground gallery on Fifth Avenue near Twenty-seventh Street to the present time, there has been a constantly flowing production of lyrical simplicity and purification. One can never think of Davies as one thinks of Courbet and of Cézanne, where the intention is first and last a technically esthetic one; especially in Cézanne, whose object was the removal of all significance from painting other than that of painting for itself. With Cézanne it was problem. One might even say it was the removal of personality. With Davies you are aware that it is an entirely intimate personal life he is presenting; a life entirely away from discussion, from all sense of problem; they are not problematic at all, his pictures; they have lyrical serenity as a basis, chiefly. Often you have the sensation of looking through a Renaissance window upon a Greek world—a world of Platonic verities in calm relation with each other. It is essentially an art created from the principle of the harmonic law in nature, things in juxtaposition, cooperating with the sole idea of a poetic existence. The titles cover the subjects, as I have suggested. Arthur B. Davies is a lyric poet with a decidedly Celtic tendency. It is the smile of a radiant twilight in his brain. It is a country of green moon whispers and of shadowed movement. Imagination illuminating the moment of fancy with rhythmic persuasiveness. It is the Pandaean mystery unfolded with symphonic accompaniment. You have in these pictures the romances of the human mind made irresistible with melodic certainty. They are *chansons sans paroles,* sung to the syrinx in Sicilian glades.

I feel that it is our own romantic land transposed into terms of classical metre. The color is mostly Greek, and the line is Greek. You could just as well hear Glück as Keats; you could just as well see the world by the light of the virgin lamp, and watch the smoke of old altars coiling among the cypress boughs. The redwoods of the West become columns of Doric eloquence and simplicity. The mountains and lakes of the West have become settings for the reading of the "Centaur" of Maurice de Guerin. You see the reason for the titles chosen because you feel that the poetry of line and the harmonic accompaniment of color is the primal essential. They are not so dynamic as suggestive in their quality of finality. The way is left open, in other words, for you yourself to wander, if you will, and possess the requisite instincts for poetry.

The presence of Arthur B. Davies, and conversation with him convince one that poetry and art are in no sense a diversion or a delusion even. They are an occupation, a real business for intelligent men and women. He is occupied with the essential qualities of poetry and painting. He is eclectic by instinct. Spiritually he arrives at his conviction through these unquestionable states of lyrical existence. He is there when they happen. That is authenticity sufficient. They are not wandering moods. They are organized conditions and attitudes, intellectually appreciated and understood. He is a mystic only in the sense that perhaps all lyrical poetry is mystic, since it strives for union with the universal soul in things.

It is perfectly autobiographical, the work of Arthur B. Davies, and that is so with all genuine expression. You find this gift for conviction in power-

ARTHUR B. DAVIES

ful painter types, like Courbet and Delacroix, who are almost propagandic in their fiercely defined insistence upon the chosen esthetic principle. Whatever emanation, illusion, or "aura," dreadful word that it is, springing from the work of Davies, is only typical of what comes from all magical intentions, the magic of the world of not-being, made real through the operation of true fancy. Davies' pictures are works of fancy, then, in contradistinction to the essays of the imagination such as those of William Blake. Poets like Davies are lookers-in. Poets like Blake are the austere residents of the country they wander in. The lookers-in are no less genuine. They merely "make" their world. It might be said they make the prosaic world over again, transform it by a system of prescribed magic. This work, then, becomes states of fancy dramatized in lyric metre. Davies feels the visionary life of facts as a scientist would feel them actually. He has the wish for absolute order and consistency. There is nothing vague or disconcerting in his work, no lapses of rhetoric. It is, in its way, complete, one may say, since it is the intelligently contrived purpose of this poet to arrive at a scheme of absolute spiritual harmony.

He is first of all the poet-painter in the sense that Albert Ryder is a painter for those with a fine comprehension of the imagination. Precisely as Redon is an artist for artists, though not always their artist in convincing esthetics, he too, satisfies the instinct for legend, for transformation. Painters like Davies, Redon, Rops, Moreau, and the other mystical natures, give us rather the spiritual trend of their own lives. In Redon and in Davies the vision is untouched by the foul breath of the world around them. In Rops and Moreau you feel the imagination hurrying to the arms and breasts of vice for their sense of home. The pathos of deliverance is urgent in them. In the work of Davies, and of Redon, there is the splendid silence of a world created by themselves, a world for the reflection of self. There is even a kind of narcissian arrogance, the enchantment of the illumined fact.

Beauty recognizing herself with satisfaction—that seems to be the purpose of the work of Arthur B. Davies. It is so much outside the realm of scientific esthetics as hardly to have been more than overheard. These pictures are efficiently exemplary of the axiom that "all art aspires to the condition of music." I could almost hear Davies saying that, as if Pater had never so much as thought of it. They literally soothe with a rare poetry painted for the eye. They are illuminations for the manuscripts of the ascetic soul. They are windows for houses in which men and women may withdraw, and be reconciled to the doom of isolation.

With the arrival of Cubism into the modern esthetic scene, there appeared a change in the manner of creation, though the same methods of invention remained chiefly without change. The result seems more in the nature of kaleidoscopic variance, a perhaps more acutely realized sense of opposites, than in the former mode. They register less completely, it seems to me, because the departure is too sudden in the rhythmus of the artist. The art of Davies is the art of a melodious curved line. Therefore the sudden angularity is abrupt to an appreciative eye.

It is the poetry of Arthur B. Davies that comes to the fore in one's appreciation. He has the almost impeccable gift for lyrical truth, and the music of motion is crystallized in his imagination to a masterful degree. He is the highly sensitized illustrator appointed by the states of his soul to picture forth the pauses of the journey through the realm of fancy. It has in it the passion of violet and silver dreaming, the hue of an endless dawn before the day descends upon the world. You expect the lute to regain its jaded tune there. You expect the harp to reverberate once again with the old fervors. You expect the syrinx to unfold the story of the reed in light song. It contains the history of all the hushed horizons that can be found over the edges of a world of materiality. It holds in it always the warm soul of every digit of the moon. Human passion is for once removed, unless it be that the mere humanism of motion excites the sense of passion. You are made to feel the non-essentiality of the stress of the flesh in the true places of spiritual existence. The life of moments is carried over and made permanent in fancy, and they endure by the purity of their presence alone. There is no violence in the work of Davies. It is the appreciable relation of harmony and counterpoint in the human heart and mind. It is the logic of rhythmical equation felt there, almost exclusively. It is the condition of music that art in the lyrical state has seemed to suggest.

The artistic versatility of Davies is too familiar to comment upon. He has no distress with mediums. His exceptional sensitivity to substance and texture gives him the requisite rapport with all species of mediums to which the artist has access. One might be inclined to think of him as a virtuoso in pastel possibly, and his paintings in the medium of oil suggest this sort of richness. He is nevertheless at home in all ways. All these are issues waved away to my mind, in view of his acute leaning to the poet that leads the artist away from problems other than that of Greek rhythmical perfection. It is essentially a Platonic expression, the desire of the perfect union of one thing with another. That is its final consummation, so it seems to me.

REX SLINKARD

"I doubt not that the passionately wept deaths of young men are provided for."—WALT WHITMAN.

WE have had our time for regretting the loss of men of genius during the war. We know the significance of the names of Rupert Brooke, Edward Thomas, Elroy Flecker on the other side of the sea, to the hope of England. And on this side of the sea the names of Joyce Kilmer, Alan Seeger and Victor Chapman have been called out to us for the poetic spell they cast upon America. All of them in their manful, poetic way. They were all of them poets in words; all but Victor Chapman were professional poets, and he, even if he himself was not aware, gave us some rare bits of loveliness in his letters. There are others almost nameless among soldier-hero people who gave us likewise real bits of unsuspected beauty in their unpretentious letters.

Rex Slinkard was a soldier, poet-painter by inclination, and ranchman as to specific occupation. Rex has gone from us, too. How many are there who know, or could have known, the magic of this unassuming visionary person. Only a few of us who understand the meaning of magic and the meaning of everlasting silences. It is the fortune of America that there remain with us numbers of highly

87

indicative drawings and a group of rare canvases, the quality of which painters will at once acclaim, and poets will at once verify the lyric perfection of, paintings and drawings among the loveliest we have in point of purity of conception and feeling for the subtle shades of existence, those rare states of life which, when they arrive, are called perfect moments in the poetic experience of men and women.

There will be no argument to offer or to maintain regarding the work of Rex Slinkard. It is what it is, the perfect evidence that one of the finest lyric talents to be found among the young creators of America has been deprived of its chance to bloom as it would like to have done, as it so eagerly and surely was already doing. Rex Slinkard was a genius of first quality. The word genius may be used these days without fear of the little banalities, since anyone who has evolved for himself a clear vision of life may be said to possess the quality of genius.

"The day's work done and the supper past. I walk through the horse-lot and to my shack. Inside I light the lantern, and then the fire, and sitting, I think of the inhabitants of the earth, and of the world, my home."

These sentences, out of a letter to a near friend, and the marginalia written upon the edges of many of his drawings, show the varying degrees of delicacy Rex was eager to register and make permanent for his own realization. His thought was once and for all upon the realities, that is, those substances that are or can be realities only to the artist, the poet, and the true dreamer, and Rex Slinkard was all of these. His observation of himself, and his understanding of himself, were uncommonly genuine in this young and so poetic painter. He had learned early for so young a man what were his special idealistic fervors. He had the true romanticist's gift for refinements, and was working continually toward the rarer states of being out from the emotional into the intellectual, through spiritual application into the proper and requisite calm. He lived in a thoroughly ordered world of specified experience which is typified in his predilection for the superiority of Chinese notions of beauty over the more sentimental rhythms of the Greeks. He had found the proper shade of intellectuality he cared for in this type of Oriental expression. It was the Buddhistic feeling of reality that gave him more than the platonic. He was searching for a majesty beyond sensuousness, by which sensuous experience is transformed into greater and more enduring shades of beauty. He wanted the very life of beauty to take the place of sensuous suggestion. Realities in place of semblances, then, he was eager for, but the true visionary realities as far finer than the materialistic reality.

He had learned early that he was not, and never would be, the fantasist that some of his earlier canvases indicate. Even his essays in portraiture, verging on the realistic, leaned nevertheless more toward the imaginative reality always. He knew, also, with clarity, the fine line of decision between imagination and vision, between the dramatic and the lyric, and had realized completely the supremacy of the lyric in himself. He was a young boy of light walking on a man's strong feet upon real earth over which there was no shadow for him. He walked straightforwardly toward the elysium of his own very personal organized fancies. His irrigation ditches were "young rivers" for him, rivers of being, across which white youths upon white horses, and white fawns were gliding to the measure of their own delights. He had, this young boy of light, the perfect measure of poetic accuracy coupled with a man's fine simplicity in him. He had the priceless calm for the understanding of his own poetic ecstasies. They acted upon him gently with their own bright pressure. He let them thrive according to their own relationships to himself. Nothing was forced in the mind and soul of Rex Slinkard. He was in quest of the modern rapture for permanent things such as is to be found in "L'après midi d'un Faun" of Mallarmé and Debussy for instance, in quest of those rare, whiter proportions of experience. It was radiance and simplicity immingled in his sense of things.

He would have served his country well as one of its clearest and best citizens, far more impressively by the growth and expansion of his soul in his own manly vision, than by the questionable value of his labors in the military service. He did what he could, gladly and heroically, but he had become too weak-ened by the siege of physical reverses that pursued his otherwise strong body to endure the strain of labor he performed, or wanted to accomplish. He knew long before he entered service the significance of discipline from very profound experience with life from childhood onward. Life had come to him voluminously because he was one who attracted life to him, electrically. He did not "whine" or "postpone," for he was in all of his hours at least mentally and spiritually equal to the world in all of its aspects. He was physically not there for the thing he volunteered to do, despite the appearance of manly strength in him, or thought he would be able to do. He hoped strongly to serve. None knew his secret so well as himself, and he kept his own secret royally and amicably.

Exceptional maturity of understanding of life, of nature, and all the little mysteries that are the shape of human moments, was conspicuously evidenced for as long as his intimates remember. The extraordinary measure of calm contained in his last pictures and in so many of the drawings done in moments of rest in camp is evidence of all this. He had a boy's brightness and certainty of the fairness of things, joined with a man's mastery of the simple problem. He was a true executive in material affairs and his vision was another part of the business of existence.

As I have said, Rex Slinkard had the priceless poise of the true lyric poet, and it was the ordered system in his vision that proved him. He knew the value of his attitudes and he was certain that perfection is imperishable, and strove with a poet's calm intensity toward that. He had found his Egypt, his Assyria, his Greece, and his own specific Nirvana at his feet everywhere.

As he stood attending to the duties of irrigation and the ripening of the alfalfa crops, he spent the moments otherwise lost in carving pebbles he found about him with rare gestures and profiles, either of his own face or body which he knew well, or the grace of other bodies and faces he had seen. He was always the young eye on things, an avid eye sure of the wonder about to escape from every living thing where light or shadow fell upon them gently. He was a sure, unquestionable, and in this sense a perfect poet, and possessed the undeniable painter's gift for presentation.

He was of the company of Odilon Redon, of whom he had never heard, in his feeling for the almost occult presence emanating from everything he encountered everywhere, and his simple letters to his friends hold touches of the same beauty his drawings and paintings and carvings on pebbles contain.

A born mystic and visionary as to the state of his soul, a boy of light in quest of the real wisdom that is necessary for the lyrical embodiment, this was Rex Slinkard, the western ranchman and poet-painter. "I think of the inhabitants of the earth and of the world, my home." This might have been a marginal note from the Book of Thel, or it might have been a line from some new songs of innocence and experience. It might have been spoken from out of one of the oaks of William Blake. It must have been heard from among the live oaks of Saugus. It was the simple speech of a ranchman of California, a real boy-man who loved everything with a poet's love because everything that lived, lived for him.

Such were the qualities of Rex Slinkard, who would like to have remained in the presence of his friends, the inhabitants of the earth, to have lived long in the world, his home.

It is all a fine clear testimony to the certainty of youth, perhaps the only certainty there can be. He was the calm declaimer of the life of everlasting beauty. He saw with a glad eye the "something" that is everywhere at all times, and in all places, for the poet's and the visionary's eye at least. He was sure of what he saw; his paintings and drawings are a firm conviction of that. Like all who express themselves clearly, he wanted to say all he had to say. At thirty he had achieved expression remarkably. He had found the way out, and the way out was toward and into the light. He was clear, and entirely unshadowed.

This is Rex Slinkard, ranchman, poet-painter, and man of the living world. Since he could not remain, he has left us a carte visite of rarest clarity and beauty. We who care, among the few, for things in relation to essences, are glad Rex Slinkard lived and laughed and wondered, and remained the little while. The new silence is but a phase of the same living one he covered all things with. He was glad he was here. He was another angle of light on the poetic world around us, another unsuspected facet of the bright surface of the world. Surfaces were for him, too, something to be "deepened" with a fresh vividness. He had the irresistible impulse to decorate and to decorate consistently. His sense of decoration was fluid and had no hint of the rhetorical in it. He felt everything joined together, shape to shape, by the harmonic insistence in life and in nature. A flower held a face, and a face held a flowery substance for him. Bodies were young trees in bloom, and trees were lines of human loveliness. The body of the man, the body of the woman, beautiful male and female bodies, the ideal forms of everyone and everything he encountered, he understood and made his own. They were all living radiances against the dropped curtain of the world. He loved the light on flesh, and the shadows on strong arms, legs, and breasts. He avoided theory, either philosophic or esthetic. He had traveled through the ages of culture in his imagination, and was convinced that nothing was new and nothing was old. It was all living and eternal when it was genuine. He stepped out of the world of visible realities but seldom, and so it was, books and methods of in-

94

terpretation held little for him. He didn't need them, for he held the whole world in his arms through the power of dream and vision. He touched life everywhere, touched it with himself.

Rex Slinkard went away into a celestial calm October 18, 1918, in St. Vincent's Hospital, New York City. It is the few among those of us who knew him as poet and visionary and man, who wish earnestly that Rex might have remained. He gave much that many wanted, or would have wanted if they had had the opportunity of knowing him. The pictures and drawings that remain are the testimony of his splendid poetic talents. He was a lyrical painter of the first order. He is something that we miss mightily, and shall miss for long.

SOME AMERICAN WATER-COLORISTS

WITH the arrival of Cézanne into the field of water-color painting, this medium suffers a new and drastic instance for comparison. It is not technical audacity alone, of course, that confronts us in these brilliantly achieved performances, so rich in form as well as radiant with light. It is not the kind of virility for its own sake that is typical of our own American artists so gifted in this special medium, like Whistler, Sargent, Winslow Homer, Dodge Macknight, John Marin, and Charles Demuth. With Cézanne it was merely a new instrument to employ for the realization of finer plastic relations. The medium of water-color has been ably employed by the English and the Dutch painters, but it seems as if the artists of both these countries succeeded in removing all the brilliance and charm as well as the freshness which is peculiar to it; few outside of Cézanne have, I think, done more with water-color than the above named American artists, none who have kept more closely and consistently within the confines and peculiarities of this medium.

In the consideration of the American water-color artists it will be found that Sargent and Homer tend always toward the graphic aspect of a pictorial idea, yet it is Homer who relieves his pictures of this obsession by a brilliant appreciation of the medium for its own sake. Homer steps out of the dry conventionalism of the English style of painting, which Sargent does not do. Much of that metallic harshness which is found in the oil pictures of Homer is relieved in the water-colors and there is added to this their extreme virtuosity, and a great distinction to be discovered in their sense of light and life, the sense of the object illumined with a wealth of vibrancy that is peculiar to its environment, particularly noticeable in the Florida series.

Dodge Macknight has seen with a keen eye the importance of this virility of technique to be found in Homer, and has added to this a passion for impressionistic veracity which heightens his own work to a point distinctly above that of Sargent, and one might almost say above Winslow Homer. Macknight really did authenticate for himself the efficacy of impression with almost incredible feats of visual bravery. There is no array of pigment sufficient to satisfy him as for what heat and cold do to his sensibility, as experienced by the opposite poles of a New England winter and a tropical Mexican landscape. He is always in search of the highest height in contrasts, all this joined by what his sense of fierceness of light could bring to the fantastic dune stretches of Cape Cod in fiery autumn. His work in water-color has the convincing charm of almost fanaticism for itself; and we find this medium progressing still further with the fearlessness of John Marin in the absolute at-home-ness which he displays on all occasions in his audacious water-color pictures.

Marin brings you to the feeling that digression is for him imperative only as affording him relief from the tradition of his medium. John Marin employs all the restrictions of water-color with the wisdom that is necessary in the case. He says that paper plus water, plus emotion will give a result in themselves and proceeds with the idea at hand in what may without the least temerity be called a masterly fashion; he has run the gamut of experience with his materials from the earliest Turner tonalities, through Whisterian vagaries on to American definiteness, and has incidentally noted that the Chinese have been probably the only supreme masters of the wash in the history of water-color painting. I can say for myself that Marin produces the liveliest, handsomest wash that is producible or that has ever been accomplished in the field of water-color painting. Perhaps many of the pictures of John Marin were not always satisfying in the tactile sense because many of them are taken up with an inevitable passion for technical virtuosity, which is no mean distinction in itself but we are not satisfied as once we were with this passion for audacity and virtuosity. We have learned that spatial existence and spatial relationships are the important essentials in any work of art. The precise ratio of thought accompanied by exactitude of emotion for the given idea is a matter of serious consideration with the modern artists of today. That is the special value of modern painting to the development of art.

The Chinese really knew just what a wash was capable of, and confined themselves to the majesty of the limitations at hand. John Marin has been wise in this also though he is not precisely fanatical, which may be his chief defect, and it is probably true that the greatest experimenters have shown fanatical tendency, which is only the accentuated spirit of obsession for an idea. How else does one hold a vision? It is the only way for an artist to produce plastic exactitude between two planes of sensation or thought. The parts must be as perfect as the whole and in the best art this is so. There must be the sense of "existence" everywhere and it might even be said that the cool hue of the intellect is the first premise in a true work of art. Virtuosity is a state of expression but it is not the final state. One must search for as well as find the sequential quality which is necessitated for the safe arrival of a work of art into the sphere of esthetic existence.

The water-colors of John Marin are restless with energy, which is in its way a real virtue. They do, I think, require, at times at least, more of the calm of research and less of the excitement of it. All true artistry is self-contained and never relies upon outer physical stimulus or inward extravagance of phantasy, or of idiosyncrasy. A work of art is never peculiar, it is always a natural thing. In this sense

99

John Marin approaches real art because he is probably the most natural water-colorist in existence.

With Charles Demuth water-color painting steps up into the true condition of ideas followed by experience. He has joined with modernism most consistently, having arrived at this state of progression by the process of investigation. The tradition of water-color painting takes a jump into the new field of modernism, and Demuth has given us his knowledge of the difference between illustration, depiction, and the plastic realization of fact. Probably no young artist has accomplished a finer degree of artistic finesse in illustration than has Charles Demuth in his series of illustrations for "The Two Magics" of Henry James, or more explicitly to say "The Turn of the Screw". These pictures are to the true observer all that could be hoped for in imaginative sincerity as well as in technical elusiveness. Demuth has since that time stepped out of the confinement of water-color pure, over into the field of tempera, which brings it nearer to the sturdier mediums employed in the making of pictures evolving a greater severity of form and a commendable rigidity of line. He has learned like so many moderns that the ruled line offers greater advantages in pictorial structure. You shall find his approach to the spirit of Christopher Wren is as clear and direct as his feeling for the vastiness of New England speechlessness. He has come up beyond the dramatisation of emotion to the point of expression for its own sake. But he is nevertheless to be included among the arrived water-colorists, because his gifts for expression have been evolved almost entirely through this medium. There is then a fine American achievement in the art of water-color painting which may safely be called at this time a localized tradition. It has become an American realization.

THE APPEAL OF PHOTOGRAPHY

PHOTOGRAPHY is an undeniable esthetic problem
upon our modern artistic horizon. The idea of
photography as an art has been discussed no doubt
ever since the invention of the pinhole. In the main,
I have always said for myself that the kodak offers
me the best substitute for the picture of life, that I
have found. I find the snapshot, almost without ex-
ception, holding my interest for what it contains of
simple registration of and adherence to facts for
themselves. I have had a very definite and plausible
aversion to the "artistic" photograph, and we
have had more than a surfeit of this sort of production for the past ten or fifteen years. I have re-
ferred frequently in my mind to the convincing portraits by David Octavius Hill as being among the
first examples of photographic portraiture to hold
my own private interest as clear and unmanipulated
expressions of reality; and it is a definite as well as
irresistible quality that pervades these mechanical
productions, the charm of the object for its own sake.
It was the irrelevant "artistic" period in photography that did so much to destroy the vital significance of photography as a type of expression
which may be classed as among the real arts of today. And it was a movement that failed because it

added nothing to the idea save a distressing super-ficiality. It introduced a fog on the brain, that was as senseless as it was embarrassing to the eye caring intensely for precision of form and accuracy of presentation. Photography was in this sense un-fortunate in that it fell into the hands of adepts at the brush who sought to introduce technical varia-tions which had nothing in reality to do with it and with which it never could have anything in common. All this sort of thing was produced in the age of the famous men and women, the period of eighteen ninety-five to nineteen hundred and ten say, for it was the age when the smart young photographer was frantic to produce famous sitters like Shaw and Rodin. We do not care anything about such things in our time because we now know that anybody well photographed according to the scope as well as the restrictions of the medium at hand could be, as has been proven, an interesting subject.

It has been seen, as Alfred Stieglitz has so clearly shown, that an eyebrow, a leg, a tree trunk, a body, a breast, a hand, any part being equal to the whole in its power to tell the story, could be made as interesting, more so indeed than all the famous people in existence. It doesn't matter to us in the least that Morgan and Richard Strauss helped fill a folio alongside of Maeterlinck and such like persons. All this was, of course, in keeping with the theatri-cism of the period in which it was produced, which is one of the best things to be said of it. But we do know that Whistler helped ruin photography along with Wilde who helped ruin esthetics. Everyone has his office nevertheless. As a consequence, Alfred Stieglitz was told by the prevailing geniuses of that time that he was a back number because of his strict adherence to the scientific nature of the medium, because he didn't manipulate his plate beyond the strictly technical advantages it offered, and it was not therefore a fashionable addition to the kind of thing that was being done by the assuming ones at that time. The exhibition of the life-work of Alfred Stieglitz in March, 1921, at the Anderson Galleries, New York, was a huge revelation even to those of us who along with our own ultra modern interests had found a place for good unadulterated photography in the scheme of our appreciation of the art production of this time.

I can say without a qualm that photography has always been a real stimulus to me in all the years I have been personally associated with it through the various exhibitions held along with those of modern painting at the gallery of the Photo-Secession, or more intimately understood as "291". Photography was an interesting foil to the kind of veracity that painting is supposed to express, or rather to say, was then supposed to express; for painting like all other ideas has changed vastly in the last ten years, and even very much since the interval created by the war. I might have learned this anywhere else, but I did get it from the Stieglitz camera realizations with more than perhaps the expected frequency, and I am willing to assert now that there are no portraits in existence, not in all the history of portrait realization either by the camera or in painting, which so definitely present, and in many instances with an almost haunting clairvoyance, the actualities existing in the sitter's mind and body and soul. These portraits are for me without parallel therefore in this particular. And I make bold with another assertion, that from our modern point of view the Stieglitz photographs are undeniable works of art, as are also the fine photographs of the younger men like Charles Sheeler and Paul Strand. Sheeler, being also one of our best modern painters, has probably added to his photographic work a different type of sensibility by reason of his experience in the so-called creative medium of painting. It is, as we know, brain matter that counts in a work of art, and we have dispensed once and for all with the silly notion that a work of art is made by hand. Art is first and last of all, a product of the intelligence.

I think the photographers must at least have been a trifle upset with this Stieglitz Exhibition. I know that many of the painters of the day were noticeably impressed. There was much to concern everyone there, in any degree that can be put upon us as interested spectators. For myself, I care nothing for the gift of interpretation, and far less for that dreadful type of effete facility which produces a kind of hocus-pocus technical brilliancy which fuddles

the eye with a trickery, and produces upon the un-
trained and uncritical mind a kind of unintelligent
hypnotism. Art these days is a matter of scientific
comprehension of reality, not a trick of the hand
or the old-fashioned manipulation of a brush or a
tool. I am interested in presentation pure and
simple. All things that are living are expression
and therefore part of the inherent symbology of life.
Art, therefore, that is encumbered with excessive
symbolism is extraneous, and from my point of
view, useless art. Anyone who understands life
needs no handbook of poetry or philosophy to tell
him what it is. When a picture looks like the life
of the world, it is apt to be a fair picture or a
good one, but a bad picture is nothing but a bad
picture and it is bound to become worse as we think
of it. And so for my own pleasure I have consulted
the kodak as furnishing me with a better picture of
life than many pictures I have seen by many of the
so-called very good artists, and I have always de-
lighted in the rotograph series of the Sunday papers
because they are as close to life as any superficial
representation can hope to be.

It was obvious then that many of those who saw
the Stieglitz photographs, and there were large
crowds of them, were non-plussed by the unmistakable authenticity of experience contained in them.
If you stopped there you were of course mystified,
but there is no mystery whatever in these productions, for they are as clear and I shall even go so far

as to say as objective as the daylight which produced them, and aside from certain intimate issues they are impersonal as it is possible for an artist to be. It is this quality in them which makes them live for me as realities in the art world of modern time. All art calls for one variety of audacity or another and so these photographs unfold one type of audacity which is not common among works of art, excepting of course in highly accentuated instances of auto-graphic revelation. It is the intellectual sympathy with all the subjects on exhibition which is revealed in these photographs: A kind of spiritual diagnosis which is seldom or never to be found among the photographers and almost never among the painters of the conventional portrait. This ability, talent, virtue, or genius, whatever you may wish to name it, is without theatricism and therefore without spec-tacular demonstration either of the sitter or the method employed in rendering them.

It is never a matter of arranging cheap and prac-tically unrelated externals with Alfred Stieglitz. I am confident it can be said that he has never in his life made a spectacular photograph. His intensity runs in quite another channel altogether. It is far closer to the clairvoyant exposure of the psychic aspects of the moment, as contained in either the persons or the objects treated of. With these essays in character of Alfred Stieglitz, you have a series of types who had but one object in mind, to lend themselves for the use of the machine in order that a certain problem might be accurately rendered with the scientific end of the process in view, and the given actuality brought to the surface when possible. I see nothing in these portraits beyond this. I understand them technically very little only that I am aware that I have not for long, and perhaps never, seen plates that hold such depths of tonal value and structural relationship of light and shade as are contained in the hundred and fifty prints on exhibition in the Anderson Galleries. Art is a vastly new problem and this is the first thing which must be learned. Precisely as we learn that a certain type of painting ended in the history of the world with Cézanne.

There is an impulse now in painting toward photographic veracity of experience as is so much in evidence in the work of an artist of such fine perceptions as Ingres, with a brushing aside of all old-fashioned notions of what constitutes artistic experience. There is a deliberate revolt, and photography as we know it in the work of Alfred Stieglitz and the few younger men like Strand and Sheeler is part of the new esthetic anarchism which we as younger painters must expect to make ourselves responsible for. It must be remembered you know, that there has been a war, and art is in a condition of encouraging and stimulating renascence, and we may even go so far as to say that it is a greater world issue than it was previous to the great catastrophe. And also, it must be heralded that as far as art is concerned the end of the world has been seen. The true artist, if he is intelligent, is witness of this most stimulating truth that confronts us. We cannot hope to function esthetically as we did before all this happened, because we are not the same beings intellectually. This does not mean in relation to photography that all straight photography is good. It merely means that the kind of photography I must name "Fifth Avenue" art, is a conspicuous species of artistic bunkum, and must be recognized as such.

Photographers must know that fogging and blurring the image is curtailing the experience of it. It is a foolish notion that mystification is of any value. Flattery is one of the false elements that enter into the making of a work of art among the artists of doubtful integrity, but this is often if not always the commercial element that enters into it. There is a vast difference between this sort of representation and that which is to be found in Greek sculpture which is nothing short of conscious plastic organization. These figures were set up in terms of the prevailing systems of proportion. Portraits were likewise "arranged" through the artistry of the painter in matters of decoration for the great halls of the periods in which they were hung. They were studies on a large scale of ornamentation. Their beauty lies chiefly in the gift of execution. In these modern photographs of Stieglitz and his followers there is an engaging directness which cannot be and must not be ignored. They do for once give in the case of the portraits, and I mean chiefly of course the Stieglitz portraits, the actuality of the sitter without pose or theatricism of any sort, a rather rare thing to be said of the modern photograph.

Stieglitz, therefore, despite his thirty or more years of experimentation comes up among the moderns by virtue of his own personal attitude toward photography, and toward his, as well as its, relation to the subject. His creative power lies in his ability to diagnose the character and quality of the sitter as being peculiar to itself, as a being in relation to itself seen by his own clarifying insight into general and well as special character and characteristic. It need hardly be said that he knows his business technically for he has been acclaimed sufficiently all over the world by a series of almost irrelevant medals and honours without end. The Stieglitz exhibition is one that should have been seen by everyone regardless of any peculiar and special predilection for art. These photos will have opened the eye and the mind of many a sleeping one as to what can be done by way of mechanical device to approach the direct charm of life in nature.

The moderns have long since congratulated Alfred Stieglitz for his originality in the special field of his own creative endeavor. It will matter little whether the ancients do or not. His product is a fine testimonial to his time and therefore this is his contribution to his time. He finds himself, and perhaps

THE APPEAL OF PHOTOGRAPHY

to his own embarrassment even, among the best modern artists; for Stieglitz as I understand him cares little for anything beyond the rendering of the problem involved which makes him of course scientific first and whatever else afterward, which is the hope of the modern artists of all movements, regardless. Incidentally it may be confided he is an artistic idol of the Dadaists which is at least a happy indication of his modernism. If he were to shift his activities to Paris, he would be taken up at once for his actual value as modern artist expressing present day notions of actual things. Perhaps he will not care to be called Dada, but it is nevertheless true. He has ridden his own vivacious hobbyhorse with as much liberty, and one may even say license, as is possible for one intelligent human being. There is no space to tell casually of his various aspects such as champion billiard player, racehorse enthusiast, etcetera. This information would please his dadaistic confrères, if no one else shows signs of interest.

SOME WOMEN ARTISTS IN MODERN PAINTING

IT is for the purpose of specialization that the term woman is herewith applied to the idea of art in painting. Art is for anyone naturally who can show degree of mastery in it. There have been a great many women poets and musicians as well as actors, though singularly enough the women painters of history have been few, and for that matter in question of proportion remain so. Whatever the wish may be in point of dismissing the idea of sex in painting, there has so often been felt among many women engaging to express themselves in it, the need to shake off marked signs of masculinity, and even brutishness of attack, as denoting, and it must be said here, a factitious notion of power. Power in painting does not come from muscularity of arm; it comes naturally from the intellect. There are a great many male painters showing too many signs of femininity in their appreciation and the conception of art in painting. Art is neither male nor female. Nevertheless, it is pleasing to find women artists such as I wish to take up here, keeping to the charm of their own feminine perceptions and feminine powers of expression. It is their very femininity which makes them distinctive in these instances. This does not imply lady-like approach or womanly attitude of moral. It merely means that their quality is a feminine quality.

In the work of Madame Delaunay Terck, who is the wife of Delaunay, the French Orphiste, which I have not seen since the war came on, one can say that she was then running her husband a very close second for distinction in painting and intelligence of expression. When two people work so closely in harmony with each other, it is and will always remain a matter of difficulty in knowing just who is the real expressor of an idea. Whatever there is of originality in the idea of Orphisme shall be credited to Delaunay as the inventor, but whether his own examples are more replete than those of Mme. Delaunay Terck is not easy of statement. There was at that time a marked increase of virility in production over those of Delaunay himself, but these are matters of private personal attack. Her Russian temper was probably responsible for this, at least no doubt, assisted considerably. There was nevertheless at that time marked evidence that she was in mastery of the idea of Orphisme both as to conception and execution. She showed greater signs of virility in her approach than did Delaunay himself. There was in his work a deal of what Gertrude Stein then called "white wind", a kind of thin escaping in the method. The designs did not lock so keenly. His work had always typical charm if it had not always satisfying vigor. His "Tour Eiffel" and a canvas called "Rugby" I think, I remember as having more grace than depth, but one may say nevertheless, real distinction.

In the exchanging of ideas so intimately as has happened splendidly between Picasso and Braque, which is in the nature of professional dignity among artists, there is bound to be more or less confusion even to the highly perceptive artist and this must therefore confuse the casual observer and layman. So it is, or was at that time with the painting of Robert Delaunay and Mme. Delaunay Terck; what you learned in this instance was that the more vigorous of the pictures were hers. She showed the same strength and style in her work as in her interesting personality which was convincing without being too strained or forced; she was most probably an average Russian woman which as one knows means a great deal as to intelligence and personal power.

MARIE LAURENCIN

With Marie Laurencin there was a greater sense of personal and individual creation. One can never quite think of anyone in connection with her pictures other than the happy reminiscence of Watteau. With her work comes charm in the highest, finest sense; there is nothing trivial about her pictures, yet they abound in all the graces of the 18th Century. Her drawings and paintings with spread fans and now and then a greyhound or a gazelle opposed against them in design, hold grace and elegance of feeling that Watteau would certainly have sanctioned. She brings up the same sense of exquisite gesture and simplicity of movement with a feeling for the romantic aspect of virginal life which exists nowhere else in modern painting. She eliminates all severities of intellect, and super-imposes wistful charm of idea upon a pattern of the most delicate beauty. She is essentially an original which means that she invents her own experience in art.

Marie Laurencin concerns herself chiefly with the idea of girlish youth, young girls gazing toward each other with fans spread or folded, and fine braids of hair tied gently with pale cerise or pale blue ribbon, and a pearl-like hush of quietude hovers over them. She arrests the attention by her fine reticence and holds one's interest by the veracity of esthetic experience she evinces in her least or greatest painting or drawing. She paints with miniature sensibility and knows best of all what to leave out. She is eminently devoid of excessiveness either in pose or in treatment, with the result that your eye is refreshingly cooled with the delicate process.

That Marie Laurencin keeps in the grace of French children is in no way surprising if you know the incomparable loveliness of them. Apart from her modernistic excellence as artist, she conveys a poetry so essentially French in quality that you wish always for more and more of it. It is the light breath of the Luxembourg gardens and the gardens of the Tuilleries coming over you once more and the same grace in child-life as existed in the costly games at Versailles among the grown-ups depicted so superbly by Watteau and his most worthy followers, Lancret and Pater, in whom touch is more breath than movement. It is a sensitive and gracefully aristocratic creation Marie Laurencin produces for us, one that makes the eye avid of more experience and the mind of more of its subtlety. It is an essentially beautiful and satisfying contribution to modern painting, this nacreous cubism of Marie Laurencin.

GEORGIA O'KEEFFE *

With Georgia O'Keeffe one takes a far jump into volcanic crateral ethers, and sees the world of a woman turned inside out and gaping with deep open eyes and fixed mouth at the rather trivial world of living people. "I wish people were all trees and I think I could enjoy them then," says Georgia O'Keeffe. Georgia O'Keeffe has had her feet scorched in the laval effusiveness of terrible experience; she has walked on fire and listened to the hissing of vapors round her person. The pictures of O'Keeffe, the name by which she is mostly known, are probably as living and shameless private documents as exist, in painting certainly, and probably in any other art. By shamelessness I mean unqualified nakedness of statement. Her pictures are essential abstractions as all her sensations have been tempered to abstraction by the too vicarious experi-

* American.—Ed.

ence with actual life. She had seen hell, one might say, and is the Sphinxian sniffer at the value of a secret. She looks as if she had ridden the millions of miles of her every known imaginary horizon, and has left all her horses lying dead in their tracks. All in quest of greater knowledge and the greater sense of truth. What these quests for truth are worth no one can precisely say, but the tendency would be to say at least by one who has gone far to find them out that they are not worthy of the earth or sky they are written on. Truth has soiled many an avenue, it has left many a drawing room window open. It has left the confession box filled with bones. However, Georgia O'Keeffe pictures are essays in experience that neither Rops nor Moreau nor Baudelaire could have smiled away.

She is far nearer to St. Theresa's version of life as experience than she could ever be to that. of Catherine the Great or Lucrezia Borgia. Georgia O'Keeffe wears no poisoned emeralds. She wears too much white; she is impaled with a white consciousness. It is not without significance that she wishes to paint red in white and still have it look like red. She thinks it can be done and yet there is more red in her pictures than any other color at present; though they do, it must be said, run to rose from ashy white with oppositions of blue to keep them companionable and calm. The work of Georgia O'Keeffe startles by its actual experience in life. This does not imply street life or sky life or drawing room life, but life in all its huge abstraction of pain and misery and its huge propensity for silencing the spirit of adventure. These pictures might also be called expositions of psychism in color and movement.

Without some one to steady her, I think O'Keeffe would not wish the company of more tangible things than trees. She knows why she despises existence, and it comes from facing the acute dilemma with more acuteness than it could comprehend. She is vastly over-size as to experience in the spiritual geometric of the world. All this gives her painting as clean an appearance as it is possible to imagine in painting. She soils nothing with cheap indulgence of wishing commonplace things. She has wished too large and finds the world altogether too small in comparison.

What the future holds for Georgia O'Keeffe as artist depends upon herself. She is modern by instinct and therefore cannot avoid modernity of expression. It is not willed, it is inevitable. When she looks at a person or a thing she senses the effluvia that radiate from them and it is by this that she gauges her loves and hates or her tolerance of them. It is enough that her pictures arrive with a strange incongruous beauty which, though metaphysically an import, does not disconcert by this insistence. She knows the psychism of patterns and evolves them with strict regard for the pictural aspects in them which save them from banality as ideas. She has no preachment to offer and utters no rubbish on the subject of life and the problem. She is one of the exceptional girls of the world both in art and in life. As artist she is as pure and free from affectation as in life she is relieved from the necessity of it.

If there are other significant women in modern art I am not as yet familiarized with them. These foregoing women take their place definitely as artists within the circle of women painters like Le Brun, Mary Cassatt, Berthe Morisot, and are in advance of them by being closer to the true appreciation of esthetics in inventing them for themselves.

REVALUATIONS IN IMPRESSIONISM

In the consideration of the real factors in the impressionistic movement, we learn that it is not Monet and the younger crew such as Moret, Maufra, George d'Espagnat and Guillaumin who give us the real weight of this esthetic argument. We find Monet going in for hyper-sentimentalized iridiscences which culminate or seem to culminate in the "Lily" series until we are forced to say he has let us out, once and for all, as far as any further interest in the theory with which he was concerned. We are no longer held by these artificial and overstrained hues, and we find the younger followers offering little or nothing to us save an obvious integrity of purpose. These younger men had apparently miscomprehended idiosyncrasies for ideas and that, save for a certain cleanness of intention, they were offering scarcely anything of what is to be found by way of realization in the pictures of a really great colorist like Renoir.

The two artists who give the true thrill of this phase of the modern movement are without question Pissarro and Sisley. It is the belief of these two artists in the appearance of things for themselves, under the influence of the light problem, which gives them a strength not always visible at first by reason of a greater simplicity of effect which dominates all of their pictures. We see in both these men a real and impressive desire for a more exacting scientific relation as discovered by intellectual consideration, than is to be found in the emotional outcry predominating in most of the pictures of Monet. These do not hold for us in this day as solidly as they were expected to. There is a kind of superficiality and consequent dissatisfaction in the conspicuous aspiration toward the first flush, one may call it, of enthusiasm for impressionistic experience. There comes to one who is really concerned, the ever increasing desire to turn toward Pissarro and Sisley and to quietly dispense with many or most of Monet's pictures, not to speak of a legitimate haste to pass over the phlegmatic enthusiasms of the younger followers.

One feels that Pissarro must have been a great man among men not so great. One feels likewise that the stately reticence of a man like Sisley is worth far more to us now, if only because we find in his works as they hang one beside another in numbers, a soberer and more cautious approach to the theme engrossing him and the other artists of the movement of that time. In the pictures of Sisley there is the charm of the fact for itself, the delight of the problem of placing the object in relation to the luminous atmosphere which covers it.

Men like Pissarro and Sisley were not forgetting Courbet and his admirable knowledge of reality.

They were not concerned with the spectacular aspect of the impressionistic principle, not nearly so much as with the satisfying realization of the object under the influence of the new scientific problem in esthetics with which they were concerned. For myself I am out of touch with Monet as a creator and I find myself extracting far more satisfaction and belief from Pissarro and Sisley, who deal with the problem of nature plus idea, with a much greater degree of let me even say sincerity, by reason of one fact and perhaps the most important one: they were not dramatizing the idea in hand. They were not creating a furor with pink and lavender haystacks. They were satisfied that there was still something to be found in the old arrangement of negative and positive tones as they were understood before the application of the spectrum turned the brains and sensibilities of men. In other words Courbet survived while the Barbizonians perished. There was an undeniable realization of fact still there, clamoring for consideration. There was the reality then even as now, as always. With Pissarro and Sisley there appeared the true separation of tone, making itself felt most intelligently in the work of these men from whom the real separatists Seurat, Signac, and Cross were to realize their principle of pointilism, of which principle Seurat was to prove himself the most satisfactory creative exponent.

The world of art lost a very great deal in the untimely death of Seurat; he was a young man of great artistic and intellectual gifts. There was an artist by the name of Vignon who came in for his share during the impressionistic period, probably not with any more dramatic glamour than he achieves now by his very simple and unpretentious pictures. I am sorry for my own pleasure that I have not been able to see more of this artist's pictures from whom I think our own Theodore Robinson must have gained a deal of strength for his own bridge building between Bastien Le Page and the Monet "eccentricity," so to call it.

There is always a reason for reticence, and it is usually apt to come from thinking. Sisley and Pissarro, Vignon, Seurat, and Robinson were thinking out a way to legitimize the new fantastic craze for prismatic violence, and they found it in the direct consideration for the fact. They knew that without objects light would have nowhere to fall, that the earth confronted them with indispensable phenomena each one of which had its reason for being. They were finding instead of losing their heads, which is always a matter of praise. I could stay with almost any Pissarro or Sisley I have ever seen, as I could always want any Seurat near me, just as I could wish almost any Monet out of sight because I find it submerged with emotional extravagance, too much enthusiasm for his new pet idea.

Scientific appreciation had not come with scientific intentions. Like most movements, it was left to other than the accredited innovators for its com-

pletion and perfection. That is why we find Cézanne working incessantly to create an art which
would achieve a union of impressionism and an art
like the Louvre, as he is said to have characterized
it for himself. We know now how much Cézanne
cared for Chardin as well as for Courbet, and Greco.
There is a reason why he must have respected Pissarro, far more than he did at any time such men as
Gaugin, the "flea on his back" as he so vividly and
perhaps justly named him. There was far more
hope for a possible great art to come out of Van
Gogh, who, in his brief seven years had experi-
mented with very aspect of impressionism that had
then been divulged. He too was in search of a
passionate realization of the object. His method of
heavy stitching in bright hues was not a perfected
style. It was an extravagant hope toward a personal
rhythm. He was an "upwardly" aspiring artist by
reason of his hyper-accentuated religious fervours.
All these extraneous and one might even say irrelevant attempts toward speedy arrivism are set aside
in the presence of the almost solemn severity of
minds like Pissarro and Sisley, and of Cézanne, who
extracted for himself all that was valuable in the
passing idea of impressionism. The picture which
lasts is never the entirely idiosyncratic one. It is
that picture which strives toward realization of ideas
through a given principle with which it is involved.
So it seems then, that if Monet invented the principle of impressionism as applied to painting, Pis-

REVALUATIONS IN IMPRESSIONISM

sarro and Sisley assisted greatly in the creative idea for our lasting use and pleasure by the consideration of the intellect which they applied to it; just as Seurat has given us a far greater realization than either Signac or Cross have offered us in the principle of pointillism.

The "test of endurance" in the impressionistic movement is borne out; the strength of realization is to be found in Pissarro and Sisley and not in the vapid niceties of Monet, whose work became thinner and thinner by habitual repetitive painting, and by a possible false sense of security in his argument. Monet had become the habitual impressionist, and the habitual in art is its most conspicuous fatality. The art of Monet grew weaker throughout the various stages of Waterloo, Venice, Rouen, Giverney, and the Water Lilies which formed periods of expression, at least to the mind of the observer. Monet's production had become a kind of mercerized production, and a kind of spurious radiance invested them, in the end. It remained for Pissarro, Sisley, Cézanne, and Seurat to stabilize the new discovery, and to give it the stamina it was meant to contain, as a scientific idea, scientifically applied.

ODILON REDON

WITH the passing of this rare artist during the late summer months,* we are conscious of the silencing of one of the foremost lyricists in painting, one of the most delicate spirits among those who have painted pictures so thoroughly replete with charm, pictures of such real distinction and merit. For of true charm, of true grace, of true melodic, Redon was certainly the master. I think no one has coveted the vision so much as, certainly no more than, has this artist, possessed of the love of all that is dreamlike and fleeting in the more transitory aspect of earthly things. No one has ever felt more that fleeting treasure abiding in the moment, no one has been more jealous of the bounty contained in the single glancing of the eye upward to infinity or downward among the minuter fragments at his feet.

It would seem as if Redon had surely walked amid gardens, so much of the morning is in each of his fragile works. There seems always to be hovering in them the breath of those recently spent dawns of which he was the eager spectator, never quite the full sunlight of the later day. Essentially he was the worshipper of the lip of flower, of dust upon the

* Of 1917.—Ed.

moth wing, of the throat of young girl, or brow of young boy, of the sudden flight of bird, the soft going of light clouds in a windless sky. These were the gentle stimulants to his most virile expression. Nor did his pictures ever contain more; they never struggled beyond the quality of legend, at least as I know them. He knew the loveliness in a profile, he saw always the evanescences of light upon light and purposeless things. The action or incident in his pictures was never more than the touch of some fair hand gently and exquisitely brushing some swinging flower. He desired implicitly to believe in the immortality of beauty, that things or entities once they were beautiful could never die, at least for him. I followed faithfully for a time these fine fragments in those corners of Paris where they could be found, and there was always sure to be in them, always and ever that perfect sense of all that is melodic in the universe.

I do not know much of his early career as an artist. I have read passages from letters which he wrote not so long ago, in which he recounts with tenderness the dream life of his childhood, how he used to stand in the field for hours or lie quietly upon some cool hill shaded with young leaves, watching the clouds transforming themselves into wing shapes and flower shapes, staining his fancy with the magic of their delicate color and form—indeed, it would seem as if all things had for him been born somewhere in the clouds and had condescended to an earthward existence for a brief space, the better to show their rarity of grace for the interval. Although obviously rendered from the object, they were still-lifes which seemed to take on a kind of cloud life during the very process of his creation. They paid tribute to that simple and unaffected statement of his—"I have fashioned an art after myself." Neither do I know just how long he was the engraver and just how long he was the painter —it is evident everywhere that his line is the line of the fastidious artist on steel and stone.

Beyond these excessively frail renderings of his, whether in oil or in pastel, I do not know him, but I am thinking always in the presence of them that he listened very attentively and with more than a common ear to the great masters in music, absorbing at every chance all that was in them for him. He had in his spirit the classical outline of music, with nothing directly revolutionary, no sign of what we call revolt other than the strict adherence to personal relationship, no other prejudice than the artist's reaction against all that is not really refined to art, with but one consuming ardor, and that to render with extreme tranquillity everything delicate and lovely in passing things. There is never anything in his pictures outside the conventional logic of beauty, and if they are at all times ineffably sweet, it is only because Redon himself was like them, joyfully living out the days because they were for him ineffably sweet, too. Most of all it is Redon who

ODILON REDON

has rendered with exceptional elegance and extreme
artistry, the fragment.

It is in his pictures, replete with exquisiteness,
that one finds the true analogy to lyric poetry. This
lyricism makes them seem mostly Greek—often I
have thought them Persian, sometimes again, Indian; certainly he learned something from the Chinese in their porcelains and in their embroidery. I
am sure he has been fond of these outer influences,
these Oriental suggestions which were for him the
spiritual equivalent from the past for his spontaneous ideas, for he, too, had much of all this magic,
as he had much of the hypnotic quality of jewelry
and precious stones in all his so delicate pictures,
firelike in their subtle brilliancy. They have always
seemed to contain this suggestion for me: flowers
that seemed to be much more the embodiment of
jades, rubies, emeralds, and ambers, than just flowers from the common garden. His flamelike
touches have always held this preciousness: notations
rather for the courtly robe or diadem than just drawings. All this gift of goldsmithery comes as one
would expect, quite naturally, from his powers as
an engraver, in which art he held a first place in his
time and was the master of the younger school,
especially in Belgium and Germany. Of all the
painters of this time it is certain he was first among
them essaying to picture the jewelled loveliness of
nature; it is most evident in La Touche who was
in no way averse to Renoir either, but Redon has

created this touch for himself and it is the touch of the virtuoso. Perhaps it would have been well if Moreau, who had a sicker love of this type of expression, had followed Redon more closely, as he might then have added a little more lustre to these very dead literary failures of his.

I cannot now say who else beside Ferdinand Khnopff has been influenced greatly by him, but I do know that he was beloved by the more modern men, that he was revered by all regardless of theories or tenets, for there is in existence somewhere in Paris a volume of letters and testimonials celebrating some anniversary of Redon in proof of it. And I think that—regardless of ideas—the artist must always find him sympathetic, if for no other reason than that he was the essence of refinement, of delicacy, and of taste. When I think of Redon I think of Shelley a little, "he is dusty with tumbling about among the stars," and I think somewhat, too, of some phrases in Debussy and his unearthly school of musicians, for if we are among those who admire sturdier things in art we can still love the fine gift of purity. And of all gifts Redon has that, certainly.

His art holds, too, something of that breathlessness among the trees one finds in Watteau and in Lancret, maybe more akin to Lancret, for he, also, was more a depicter of the ephemeral. We think of Redon as among those who transvaluate all earthly sensations in terms of a purer element. We think of him as living with his head among the mists, alert for all those sudden bursts of light which fleck here and there forgotten or unseen places, making them live with a new resplendency, full of new revealment, perfect with wonder. Happily we find in him a hatred of description and of illustration, we find these pictures to be illuminations from rich pages not observed by the common eye, decorations out of a world the like of which has been but too seldom seen by those who aspire to vision. *Chansons sans paroles* are they, ringing clearly and flawlessly to the eye as do those songs of Verlaine (with whom he has also some relationship) to the well-attuned ear.

He was the master of the nuance, and the nuance was his lyricism, his special gift, his genius. He knew perfectly the true vibration of note to note, and how few are they whose esthetic emotions are built upon the strictly poetic basis, who escape the world-old pull towards description and illustration. How few, indeed, among those of the materialistic vision escape this. But for Redon there was but one world, and that a world of imperceptible light on all things visible, with always a kind of song of adoration upon his lips, as it were, obsessed with reverence and child wonder toward every least and greatest thing, and it was in these portrayals of least things that he exposed their naked loveliness as among the greatest. Never did Redon seek for the miniature; he knew merely that the part is the representation of the whole, that the perfect fragment is a true representative of beauty, and that the vision of some fair hand or some fair eye is sure to be the epitome of all that is lovely in the individual.

We have as a result of this almost religious devotion of Redon's, the fairest type of the expression of that element which is the eye's equivalent for melodious sound. In his pictures he perpetuated his belief in the unfailing harmony in things. Either all things were lovely in his eye, or they are made beautiful by thinking beautifully of them. That was the only logic in Redon's painting. He questioned nothing; he saw the spiritual import of every object on which his eye rested. No one shall go to Redon for any kind of intellectual departure or for any highly specialized theory—it is only too evident from his work that he had none in mind. He had, I think, a definite belief in the theosophic principle of aura, in tnat element of emanation which would seem sometimes to surround delicate objects touched with the suffusion of soft light. For him all things seemed "possessed" by some colorful presence which they themselves could in no way be conscious of, somewhat the same sort of radiance which floods the features of some beauteous person and creates a presence there which the person is not even conscious of, the imaginative reality, in other words, existing either within or without everything the eye beholds. For him the very air which hovered about all things seemed to have, as well, the presence of color not usually seen of men, and it was this emanation or presence which formed the living quality of his backgrounds in which those wondrous flowery heads and hands and wings had their being, through which those dusty wings of most unearthly butterflies or moths hurry so feverishly. He has given us a happy suggestion of the reality of spiritual spaces and the way that these fluttering bodies which are little more than spirit themselves have enjoyed a beauteous life. He was Keats-like in his appreciation of perfect loveliness, like Shelley in his passionate desire to transform all local beauty into universal terms.

No one will quarrel with Redon on account of what is not in him. What we do find in him is the poetry of a quiet, sweet nature in quest always of perfect beauty, longing to make permanent by means of a rare and graceful art some of those fragments which have given him his private and personal clue to the wonders of the moment, creating a personal art by being himself a rare and lovely person. He remains for us one of the finest of artists, who has reverted those whisperings from the great world of visual melody in which he lived. It was with these exquisite fragments that he adorned the states of his own soul in order that he might present them as artist in tangible art form. We are grateful for his lyricism and for his exquisite goldsmithery. After viewing his delicately beautiful pictures, objects take on a new poetic wonder.

THE VIRTUES OF AMATEUR PAINTING

WITH SPECIAL PRAISES FOR JENNIE VANVLEET
COWDERY

SOME of the finest instances of pure painting will be found, not as might be imagined by the layman, among the professional artists, but among those amateurs whose chief occupation is amusing themselves first of all. If you who read will make close reference to those rich examples of the mid-Victorian period, when it was more or less distinguished to take up painting along with the other accomplishments, you will find that the much tabooed antimacassar period produced a species of painting that was as indicative of personal style and research as it was fresh in its elemental approach. The perfect instance in modern art of this sort of original painting raised to the highest excellence is that of Henri Rousseau, the true primitive of our so eclectic modern period. No one can have seen a picture of this most talented douanier without being convinced that technique for purely private personal needs has been beautified to an extraordinary degree.

Rousseau stands among the very best tonalists as well as among the best designers of modern time, and his pictures hold a quality so related to the experience contained in their subjects, as to seem like

134

the essence of the thing itself. You feel that unquestionably Rousseau's Paris is Paris, and you are made to feel likewise that his jungle scenes are at very least his own experiences of his earlier life in Mexico. Rousseau convinces by his unquestionable sensitivity and integrity of approach. He was not fabricating an art, he was endeavoring to create a real picture for his own private satisfaction, and his numerous successes are both convincing and admirable.

As I have said, if you have access to a variety of amateur pictures created during the mid-Victorian era, of whatever style or subject, you will find in them the most admirably sincere qualities of painting as well as singularly enchanting gifts for simplication and the always engaging respect for the fact itself out of which these painted romanzas are created. There was the type of memorial picture for instance, with its proverbial tombstone, its weeping willow tree, and its mourner leaning with one elbow, usually on the cornice above, where the name of the beloved deceased is engraved; below it the appropriate motto and its added wealth of ornamentation in the way of landscape, with houses, hills, winding roads, with maybe an animal or two grazing in the field, and beyond all this vista, an ocean with pretty vessels passing on their unmindful way, and more often than not, many species of bright flowers in the foreground to heighten the richness of memory and the sentimental aspects of bereavement.

I wish I could take you to two perfect examples of this sort of amateur painting which I have in mind, now in the possession of the Maine Historical Society, of Portland, Maine, as well as one other superb and still more perfect example of this sort of luxuriously painted memory of life, in the collection of a noted collector of mid-Victorian splendours, near Boston. It is sensation at first hand with these charmingly impressive amateur artists. They have been hampered in no way with the banality of school technique learned in the manner of the ever-present and unoriginal copyist. They literally invent expression out of a personally accumulated passion for beauty and they have become aware of it through their own intensely personalised contact with life. The marine painters of this period, and earlier, of which there have been almost numberless instances, and of whose fine performances there are large numbers on view in the Marine Museum in Salem, Mass., offer further authentication of private experience with phases of life that men of the sea are sure to know, the technical beauty alone of which furnishes the spectator with many surprises and fascinations in the line of simplicity and directness of expression.

Many of these amateur painters were no longer young in point of actual years. Henri Rousseau was as we know past forty when he was finally driven to painting in order to establish his own psychic entity. And so it is with all of them, for there comes a certain need somewhere in the consciousness of everyone, to offset the tedium of common experience with some degree of poetic sublimation. With the result that many of them find their way out by taking to paints and brushes and canvas, astonishing many a real painter, if not the untutored layman, who probably expects to be mystified in one way or another by something which he thinks he does not understand. It is of the charming pictures of Jennie Vanvleet Cowdery that I wish to speak here.

Mrs. Cowdery is a southern lady, and of this fact you become aware instantly you find yourself in conversation with her. She evidences all the traits and characteristics of a lady of her period, which is to say the late mid-Victorian, for she must have been a graceful young woman herself at the close of this fascinating period. And you find, therefore, in her quaint and convincingly original pictures, the passion for the charms and graces that were consistent with the period in which she spent her girlhood, and which has left upon her consciousness so dominant a trace. The pictures of Mrs. Cowdery, despite their remoteness of surrounding—for she always places her graceful figures, which are no less than the embodiments of her own graceful states of being, in a dense woodland scene—bring up to the senses all the fragrances of that past time, the redolence of the oleander by the wall, of the camelia in the shadow, and of the pansy by the hedge. You expect these ladies to shake gently upon the air, like flowers in the morning, their own fascinating perfumes, as you expect them to recite in the quietude of the wood in which they are walking those sentiments which are appropriate to the season and of other soft remembrances.

Mrs. Cowdery might have taken to needlework, and sat like many another young woman of that time by the window with the sunlight streaming in upon the coloured stitches of her work, or she might perhaps more strictly have taken to miniature painting, the quality of which style is so much in evidence in these pleasant pictures of hers. The pictures of Mrs. Cowdery will not stimulate the spectator to reflect with gravity upon the size of the universe, but they dwell entirely upon the intimate charm of it, the charm that rises out of breeding and cultivation, and a feeling for the finer graces of the body and sweet purities of mind. Mrs. Cowdery is essentially a breather and a bringer of peace. There is no purpose in these gracious and entertaining pictures, for they are invented solely to recall and make permanent, for this lady's own delight, those moments of joy of which there must have been many if the gentleness and the clear quality of revery in them is to be taken; and these pictures are to be taken first and last as genuine works of art in their own way, which is the only way that true works of art can be taken seriously.

The most conspicuous virtue of these quaintly engaging pictures of Mrs. Cowdery is the certainty you find in them of the lack of struggle. Their author is, without doubt, at peace with the world, for the world is without significance in the deeper sense to all really serious artists, those who have vital information to convey. Mrs. Cowdery's career as a painter is of short and impressive duration, barely four years she confides, and she has been an engaging feature of the Society of Independent Artists for at least three of these years, I believe. It is her picture which she names "1869" which has called most attention to her charming talents, and which created so convincing an impression among the artists for its originality and its insistence upon the rendering of beautified personal experience.

Mrs. Cowdery must have loved her earliest girlish hours with excessive delight, and perhaps it is the garish contrast of the youth of the young women of this time, energetic and, from the mid-Victorian standpoint certainly, so unwomanly, that prompts this gentle and refined woman to people her gracious solitudes of spirit with those still more gracious ladylike beings which she employs. For her pictures, that is her most typical ones, contain always these groupings of figures in crinoline-like gowns with perhaps more of the touch of eighteen-eighty than of seventy in them, so given to flounces and

cascades of lace with picture hats to shade the eyes,
and streamers of velvet ribbon to give attenuated
sensations of grace to their quietly sweeping figures that seem to be always in a state of harmless
gossip among themselves. One never knows
whether it is to be quite morning or afternoon for
there is seldom or never present the quality of direct sunlight; but as ladies and gentlemen usually
walk in the afternoon even now, if there are still
such virtuous entities as ladies and gentlemen, we
may presume that these are afternoon seances,
poetically inscribed, which Mrs. Cowdery wishes to
convey to us. That Mrs. Cowdery has a well adjusted feeling for the harmony of hues is evident
in her production as well as in the outline of her
simple and engaging conversation.

Thus the lady lives, in a world gently fervorous
with lyric delicacies, and her own almost girlish
laughter is like a kind of gracious music for the
scenes she wishes to portray. I am reminded in this
instance to compare her gentle voice with the almost
inaudible one of Albert Ryder, that greatest of
visionaries which America has so far produced. It
is probable that all mystical types have voices softened to whispers by the vastness of the experience
which they have endured. These gentle souls survive the period they were born in, and it is their
clean and unspoiled vision that brings them over to
us in this hectic and metallic era of ours. They
come, it must be remembered, from the era of Jenny

THE VIRTUES OF AMATEUR PAINTING

Lind and Castle Garden, though of course in Mrs. Cowdery's case she is too young actually to have survived that period literally. It is the grace of that period, however, to which she has become heir and all her efforts have been exercised in rendering of the graces of this playful and pretty hour of human life.

We are reminded, for the moment only, of Monticelli, chiefly through similarity of subject, for he also was fond of the silent park inhabited with gracious beings in various states of spiritual ecstasy and satisfaction. In the pictures of Mrs. Cowdery there is doubtless greater intimacy of feeling, because it is a private and very personal issue with her own happy soul. She has come out on the other edge of the horizon of the world of humans, and finds the looking backward so imperatively exquisite as to make it necessary for her to paint them with innocent fidelity; and so she has set about, without any previous experience in the handling of homely materials, to make them tell in quaint and gracious accents the pretty story of the life of her revivified imagination. In these ways she becomes a kind of revivification of the spirit of Watteau, who has made perfect, for us all, what is perfect in the classicized ideality of experience.

I think of Mrs. Cowdery's pictures as mid-Victorian fans, for they seem more like these frail shapes to be wafted by frail and slender hands; I seem to feel the quiet glitter of prisms hanging from

huge chandeliers in a ball-room, as I look at them;
for they become, if you do not scrutinize them too
closely as works of art, rather as prismatic memories
bathed in the light of that other time, when men
and women now grandfathers and grandmothers
were young and handsome boys and girls, seeking
each other out in the fashion of polite beaus and
belles, a period that will never come again, it is certain. Mrs. Cowdery need not be alarmed that
modern painters wish to offer plain homage to her
fresh and engaging talents. It is an object lesson,
if such is necessary, to all men and women past fifty:
that there is still something for each of them to do
in a creative way; and I can think of no more engaging way for them than to recite the romantic
history of their youthful longings and realizations
to a world that has little time for making history
so romantically inoffensive.

Mrs. Cowdery may be complimented therefore
that she has followed her professional daughter's
advice to take up painting as a pastime, and she has
already shown in these brief four years, with all
the intermissions that are natural to any ordinary
life, that she is a fine type of amateur artist with all
the world of rediscovery at her disposal. She will
be hampered in no way with the banalities of in-
struction offered her by the assuming ones. She
is beyond the need of anything but self-invention,
and this will be her own unique and satisfying pleasure. It is in no way amiss, then, to congratulate

THE VIRTUES OF AMATEUR PAINTING

Mrs. Cowdery upon her new and vital artistic career. That she will have further success is proven by the few pictures already created by her. They show the unmistakable signs of taste and artistic comprehension as applied to her own spiritual vision. No intervention will be of any avail, save perhaps the permissible intervention of praise and congratulations.

Incidentally, I would recommend to those artists who are long since jaded with repetition and success, and there are many of them, to refresh their eyes and their senses with the work of these outwardly unassuming but thoroughly convincing amateurs, like Henri Rousseau, Mrs. Cowdery and the many others whose names do not appear on their handsome works of art. There is such freshness of vision and true art experience contained in them. They rely upon the imagination entirely for their revelations, and there is always present in these unprofessional works of art acute observation of fact and fine gifts for true fancy. These amateurs are never troubled with the "how" of mediocre painting; neither are they troubled with the wiles of the outer world. They remain always charming painters of personal visionary experience, and as such are entitled to praise for their genuine gifts in rendering, as well as for a natural genius for interpretation.

HENRI ROUSSEAU

NOT long since, we heard much of naïveté—it was the fashion among the schools and the lesser individuals to use this term in describing the work of anyone who sought to distinguish himself by eccentricity of means. It was often the term applied to bizarrerie—it was fashionable to draw naïvely, as it was called. We were expected to believe in a highly developed and overstrained simplicity, it was the resort of a certain number who wanted to realize speedy results among the unintelligent. It was a pose which lasted not long because it was obviously a pose, and a pose not well carried, it had not the prescribed ease about it and showed signs of labor. It had, for a time, its effect upon really intelligent artists with often respectable results, as it drew the tendency away from too highly involved sophistication. It added a fresh temper in many ways, and helped men to a franker type of self-expression; and was, as we may expect, something apart from the keen need of obliviousness in the great modern individualists, those who were seeking direct contact with subject.

We have learned in a short space of time that whatever was exceptional in the ideas and attitudes of the greater ones, as we know them, was not at all the outcome of the struggle toward an affected naïveté such as we have heard so much about, but was, on another hand, a real phase of their originality, the other swing of the pendulum, so to call it. It was the "accent" of their minds and tempers, it was a true part of their personal gesture, and was something they could not, and need not, do anything about, as if it were the normal tendency in them in their several ways. We all of us know that modern art is not haphazard, it is not hit or miss in its intention at least, certainly not the outcome of oddity, of whim, or of eccentricity, for these traits belong to the superficial and cultivated. We have found that with the best moderns there has been and is inherent in them the same sincerity of feeling, the same spirit directing their research. The single peculiarity of modern art therefore, if such there be, is its special relationship to the time in which it is being produced, explicitly of this age.

What we know of the men, much or little, proves that they are, and have all been, simple earnest men, intelligent, following nowise blindly in pursuit of fresh sensation, excitement, a mere phantasy, or freak of the mind. It was, and is, the product of a logic essentially of themselves, and of the period they represent; and because this period is not the period of sentimentality in art, but a period striving toward a more vigorous type of values—something as beautiful as the machinery of our time—it is not as yet to any great degree cared for, understood nor, up to very recently, even trusted. It has destroyed old fashioned romance, and the common eye has ceased to focus, or rather, does not wish to concentrate on things which do not visualize the literary sensation. In the midst of all this struggle was Henri Rousseau, the real and only naif of this time, and certainly among the truest of all times. As much as a man can remain child, Rousseau remained the child, and as much as a man could be naïve and childlike, certainly it was this simple artist who remained so.

If report has the truth correctly, Rousseau began his career as painter at the age of forty, though it is quite possible and probable that he was painting whenever he could, in his untutored fashion, in all of his spare intervals, and with but one object in view apparent: to give forth in terms of painting those phases of his own personal life which remained indelibly impressed upon his memory, pictorially always vivid to him, as in his pictures they are seen to be the scenes or incidents of loveliness to his fine imagination. We find them covering a rather wide range of experience, apparently in two places, somewhere in the tropics of Mexico, and Paris; the former, experiences of youth in some sort of governmental service I believe, and the latter, the more intimate phases of life about him in Paris, of Paris herself and of those people who created for him the intimacy of his home life, and the life which

146

centered about the charming rue de Perelle where
he lived.

In Rousseau then, we have one of the finest individual expressions of the amateur spirit in painting,
taking actually a place among the examples of paintings, such as those of the Kwakiutl Indians, or the
sculpture of the Congo people, partaking of the
very same quality of directness and simplicity, and
of contact with the prevailing image chosen for representation. He was too evidently the product of
himself, he was not hybrid, nor was he in any sense
something strange springing up out of the soil in
the dark of night, he was not mushroom. He did
not know the meaning of affectation, and I doubt
if he even knew what was meant by simplicity, so
much was he that element himself.

It is with fascination that we think of him as
living his life out after his discharge for incompe-
tency from the customs service outside the fortifica-
tions of Paris, and doubtless with the strain of pov-
erty upon him also, within a ten minutes' walk from
the world famous quartiers, and almost certainly
knowing nothing of them. That there was a
Julian's or a Colarossi's anywhere about, it is not
likely that he knew, or if he knew, not more than
vaguely. He drew his quaint inspirations directly
from the sources of nature and some pencil drawings
I have seen prove the high respect and admiration,
amounting to love and worship, which he had for

nature and the phenomena of her, to be disclosed at every hedge.

If he was no success as a douanier, he was learning a great deal, meanwhiles, about those delicate and radiant skies which cover Paris at all times, charming always for their lightness and delicacy, pearl-like in their quiet splendour; and it was during this service of his at the city's gates that he learned his lovely sense of blacks and greys and silvers, of which Paris offers so much always, and which predominate in his canvases. Even his tropical scenes strive in no way toward artificiality of effect, but give rather the sense of their profundity than of oddity, of their depth and mystery than of peculiarity. He gives us the sense of having been at home in them in his imagination, being so well at home in those scenes of Paris which were daily life to him. We find in Rousseau true naïveté, without struggle, real child-likeness of attitude and of emotion, following diligently with mind and with spirit the forms of those stored images that have registered themselves with directness upon the area of his imagination, never to be forgotten, rendered with perfect simplicity for us in these quaint pictures of his, superb in the richness of quality which makes of them, what they are to the eye that is sympathetic to them, pictures out of a life undisturbed by all the machinations and intrigues of the outer world, a life intimate with itself, remote from all agencies having no direct association with it, living with a

HENRI ROUSSEAU

sweet gift of enchantment with the day's disclo-
sures, occupied apparently with nothing beyond the
loveliness contained in them.

There is not once, anywhere, a striving of the
mind in the work of this simple man. It was a
wealth of innocence that tinged all his methods, and
his pictures are as simple in their appeal as are the
declarations of Jacob Boehme—they are the songs
of innocence and experience of a nature for whom
all the world was beautiful, and have about them
the element of song itself, a poetry that has not yet
reached the shaping of words. Who looks at the
pictures of this true and charming naif, will find
nothing to wonder at beyond this extreme simplicity,
he had no prescribed attitude, no fixity of image that
characterizes every touch of school. He was taught
only by nature and consulted only her relationships
and tendencies. There is never a mistaking of that.
Nature was his influence, and he saw with an. un-
trammelled eye the elemental shape of all things,
and affixed no falsity of feeling, or anything, to
his forms which might have detracted from their extreme simplicity. He had "first sight," first contact
with the image, and sought nothing else beyond this,
and a very direct correspondence with memories dic-
tated all his efforts.

That Rousseau was musical, is shown in the natural grace of his compositions, and his ideas were
simple as the early songs of France are simple,
speaking of everyday things with simple heart and

149

voice, and he painted frankly what he saw in precisely the way he saw it. We, who love richness and sobriety of tone, will never tire of Rousseau's beautiful blacks and greys, and probably no one has excelled them for delicacy of appreciation, and perfection of gradation. It will be long before the landscapes will be forgotten, it will be long before the exquisite portrait of the "Child with the Harlequin" will fade from remembrance, we shall remember them all for their loveliness in design, a gift which never failed him, no matter what the subject. Simple arabesque, it was the jungle that taught him this, and therein lay his special power, a genuine feeling for the richness of laces and brocades in full and subdued tones, such as one would find in the elaborate intricacies of tropical foliage, strange leaves intermingled with parrots, monkeys, strange white lilies on high stalks, tigers peering through highly ornate foliage and branches intertwined, all excellently suggestive of that foreign land in which the mind wanders and finds itself so much at home.

"Le Charmeur," "Jadwigha," in these are concentrated all that is lovely in the land of legend; and, like all places of legend, replete with imaginative beauty, the places where loveliness and beauty of form congregate, after they have passed through the sensuous spaces of the eye travelling somewhere to an abode where all those things are that are perfect, they live forever. Rousseau was a charming and lovable child, whether he was painting or whether he was conducting his own little orchestra, composed of those people who kept shop around his home, and it is as the child of his time that he must be considered, child in verity among the sophisticated moderns who believed and believe more in intellect than in anything else, many of whom paid tribute to him, and reverenced him, either in terms of sincere friendship, or by occasional visit. The various anecdotes, touching enough, are but further proof of the innocence of this so simple and untutored person.

The real amateur spirit has, we like to think, much in its favor, if only for its freshness, its spontaneity, and a very gratifying naturalness. Rousseau was all of this, and lived in a world untouched, he wove about himself, like other visionaries, a soft veil hiding all that was grossly unreal to him from all that was real, and for Rousseau, those things and places he expressed existed vividly for him, and out of them his pictures became true creations. He was the real naif, because he was the real child, unaffected and unspoiled, and painting was for him but the key of heaven that he might open another door for the world's weary eye.

PART TWO

THE TWILIGHT OF THE ACROBAT

WHERE is our once charming acrobat—our minstrel of muscular music? What has become of these groups of fascinating people gotten up in silk and spangle? Who may the evil genius be who has taken them and their fascinating art from our stage, who the ogre of taste that has dispensed with them and their charm? How seldom it is in these times that one encounters them, as formerly when they were so much the charming part of our lighter entertainment. What are they doing since popular and fickle notions have removed them from our midst?

It is two years since I have seen the American stage. I used to say to myself in other countries, at least America is the home of real variety and the real lover of the acrobat. But I hear no one saying much for him these days, and for his charming type of art.

What has become of them all, the graceful little lady of the slack wire, those charming and lovely figures that undulate upon the air by means of the simple trapeze, those fascinating ensembles and all the various types of melodic muscular virtuosity?

We have been given much, of late, of that virtuosity of foot and leg which is usually called dancing; and that is excellent among us here, quite the contribution of the American, so singularly the prodduct of this special physique. Sometimes I think there are no other dancers but Americans. It used to be so delightful a diversion watching our acrobat and his group with their strong and graceful bodies writhing with rhythmical certitude over a bar or upon a trapeze against a happily colored space. Now we get little more in the field of acrobatics beyond a varied buck and wing; everything seems tuxedoed for drawing room purposes. We get no more than a decent handspring or two, an overelaborated form of split. It all seems to be over with our once so fashionable acrobat. There is no end of good stepping, as witness the Cohan Revue, a dancing team in Robinson Crusoe, Jr., and "Archie and Bertie" (I think they call themselves). This in itself might be called the modern American school: the elongated and elastic gentleman who finds his co-operator among the thin ones of his race, artistically speaking. I did not get to the circus this year, much to my regret; perhaps I would have found my lost genius there, among the animals disporting themselves in less charitable places. But we cannot follow the circus naturally, and these minstrel folk are disappearing rapidly. Variety seems quite to have given them up and replaced them with often very tiresome and mediocre acts of singing.

How can one forget, for instance, the Famille Bouvier who used to appear regularly at the fêtes

THE TWILIGHT OF THE ACROBAT

in the streets of Paris in the summer season, living all of them in a roving gipsy wagon as is the custom of these fête people. What a charming moment it was always to see the simple but well built Mlle. Jeanne of twenty-two pick up her stalwart and beautifully proportioned brother of nineteen, a strong, broad-shouldered, manly chap, and balance him on one hand upright in the air. It was a classic moment in the art of the acrobat, interesting to watch the father of them all training the fragile bodies of the younger boys and girls to the systematic movement of the business while the mother sat in the doorway of the caravan nursing the youngest at the breast, no doubt the perfect future acrobat. And how charming it was to look in at the doors of these little houses on wheels and note the excellent domestic order of them, most always with a canary or a linnet at the curtained window and at least one cat or dog or maybe both. This type is the progenitor of our stage acrobat, it is the primitive stage of these old-time troubadours, and it is still prevalent in times of peace in France. The strong man gotten in tawdry pink tights and much worn black velvet with his very elaborate and drawn out speeches, in delicate French, concerning the marvels of his art and the long wait for the stipulated number of *dix centimes* pieces before his marvellous demonstration could begin. This is, so to say, the vagabond element of our type of entertainment, the wandering minstrel who keeps generation after generation to the art of his forefathers, this fine old art of the pavement and the open country road. But we look for our artist in vain these days, those groups whose one art is the exquisite rhythmical display of the human body, concerted muscular melody. We cannot find him on the street in the shade of a stately chestnut tree as once in Paris we found him at least twice a year, and we seek him in vain in our modern music hall.

Is our acrobatic artist really gone to his esthetic death; has he 'given his place permanently to the ever present singing lady who is always telling you who her modiste is, sings a sentimental song or two and then disappears; to the sleek little gentleman who dances off a moment or two to the tune of his doll-like partner whose voice is usually littler than his own? Perhaps our acrobat is still the delight of those more characteristic audiences of the road whose taste is less fickle, less blasé. This is so much the case with the arts in America—the fashions change with the season's end and there is never enough of novelty; dancing is already dying out, skating will not prevail for long among the idle; what shall we predict for our variety which is in its last stages of boredom for us?

I suspect the so-called politeness of vaudeville of the elimination of our once revered acrobats. The circus notion has been replaced by the parlor entertainment notion. Who shall revive them for us, who admire their simple and unpretentious art; why is there not someone among the designers with sufficient interest in this type of beauty to make attractive settings for them, so that we may be able to enjoy them at their best, which in the theater we have never quite been able to do—designs that will in some way add luster to an already bright and pleasing show of talents.

I can see, for instance, a young and attractive girl bareback rider on a cantering white horse inscribing wondrous circles upon a stage exquisitely in harmony with herself and her white or black horse as the case might be; a rich cloth of gold backdrop carefully suffused with rose. There could be nothing handsomer, for example, than young and graceful trapezists swinging melodically in turquoise blue doublets against a fine peacock background or it might be a rich pale coral—all the artificial and spectacular ornament dispensed with. We are expected to get an exceptional thrill when some dull person appears before a worn velvet curtain to expatiate with inappropriate gesture upon a theme of Chopin or of Beethoven, ideas and attitudes that have nothing whatsoever to do with the musical intention; yet our acrobat whose expression is certainly as attractive, if not much more so generally, has always to perform amid fatigued settings of the worst sort against red velvet of the most depraved shade possible. We are tired of the elaborately costumed person whose charms are trivial and insignificant, we are well tired also of the ordinary gentleman dancer and of the songwriter, we are bored to extinction by the perfectly dull type of playlet which features some well known legitimate star for illegitimate reasons. Our plea is for the re-creation of variety into something more conducive to light pleasure for the eye, something more conducive to pleasing and stimulating enjoyment. Perhaps the reinstatement of the acrobat, this revival of a really worthy kind of expression, would effect the change, relieve the monotony. The argument is not too trivial to present, since the spectator is that one for whom the diversion is provided.

I hear cries all about from people who once were fond of theater and music hall that there is an inconceivable dullness pervading the stage; the habitual patron can no longer endure the offerings of the present time with a degree of pleasure, much less with ease. It has ceased to be what it once was, what its name implies. If the old school inclined toward the rough too much, then certainly the new inclines distressingly toward the refined—the stage that once was so full of knockabout is now so full of stand-still; variety that was once a joy is now a bore. Just some uninteresting songs at the piano before a giddy drop is not enough these days; and there are too many of such. There is need of a greater activity for the eye. The return of the acrobat in a more modern dress would be the appropriate acquisition, for we still have appreciation

THE TWILIGHT OF THE ACROBAT

for all those charming geometrics of the trapeze, the bar, and the wire.

It is to be hoped that these men will return to us, stimulating anew their delightful kind of poetry of the body and saving our variety performances from the prevailing plague of monotone.

VAUDEVILLE

I HAVE but recently returned from the vaudeville of the centuries. Watching the kick and the glide of very ancient performers. I have spent a year and a half down in the wonderful desert country of the Southwest. I have wearied, however, of the ancient caprice, and turn with great delight to my old passion, vaudeville. I return with glee to the ladies and gentlemen and pet animals of the stage, including the acrobats. Is there one who cares for these artists and for their rhythmical gesture more than myself? I cannot think so. I have wished with a real desire to create new sets for them, to establish an altogether new tradition as regards the background of these charming artists. If that were the chosen field for my esthetic activities, I should be famous by now for the creation of sets and drops by which these exceptional artists might make a far more significant impression upon the type of public they essay to interest and amuse.

I would begin first of all by severing them from the frayed traditions of worn plush and sequin, rid them of the so inadequate back drop such as is given them, the scene of Vesuvius in eruption, or the walk in the park at Versailles. They need first of all large plain spaces upon which to perform, and enjoy their own remarkably devised patterns of body. I speak of the acrobats, the animals, the single and double dancers who perform "down in one" more especially. The so called headliners have their plush parlours with the inevitable purple or rose lamp, and the very much worn property piano just barely in tune. Only the dressmaker and the interior decorator can do things for them, as we see in the case of Kitty Gordon. It is to be hoped that a Beardsley of the stage will one day appear and really do something for the dainty type of person or the superbly theatric artist such as Miss Gordon, Valeska Suratt, and the few other remarkable women of the vaudeville stage.

I am more concerned with the less appreciated artists. I would see that they glitter by their own brilliance. Why, for instance, should a fine act like the Four Danubes and others of their quality be tagged on to the end of a bill, at which time the unmannerly public decides to go home or hurry to some roof or other, or dining place?

I should like seeing the Brothers Rath likewise, perhaps as refined acrobatic artists as have been seen on our stage for some time, in a set that would show them to better advantage, and give the public a greater intimacy with the beauty of their act than can be had beyond the first six rows of the Winter Garden. They are interposed there as a break between burlesques, which is not the place for them. I would "give" them the stage while they are on it. Theirs is a muscular beauty which has not been excelled. I have no doubt that if I attempted to establish these ideas with the artists whom I spend so much time in championing, they would no doubt turn aside with the word "highbrow" on their lips. They would have to be shown that they need these things, that they need the old-fashioned ideas removed, and fresher ones put in their place. I have expressed this intention once before in print, perhaps not so vehemently. I should like to elaborate. I want a Metropolitan Opera for my project. An orchestra of that size for the larger concerted groups, numbers of stringed instruments for the wirewalkers and jugglers, a series of balanced woodwinds for others, and so on down the line, according to the quality of the performer. There should be a large stage for many elephants, ponies, dogs, tigers, seals. The stage should then be made more intimate for the solos, duets, trios, and quartets among the acrobats. I think a larger public should be made aware of the beauty and skill of these people, who spend their lives in perfecting grace and power of body, creating the always fascinating pattern and form, orchestration if you will, the orchestration of the muscles into a complete whole. You will of course say, go to the circus, and get it all at once. The circus is one of the most charming places in existence, because it is one of the last words in orchestrated physical splendour. But the circus is too diffused, too enormous in this country to permit of concentrated interest, attention, or pleasure. One goes away with many little bits. It is because the background is made up of restless nervous dots, all anxious to get the combined quota which they have paid for, when in reality they do not even get any one thing. It is the alert eye which can go over three rings and two stages at once and enjoy the pattern of each of them. It is a physical impossibility really.

I think we should be made aware in finer ways of the artists who open and close our bills. Why must the headliner always be a talking or a singing person who tells you how much money he needs, or how much she is getting? There is more than one type of artistic personality for those who care for vaudeville. Why doesn't a team like the Rath Brothers, for example, find itself the feature at‹ traction? Must there always be the string of unnecessary little men and women who have. such a time trying to fill up their twenty-two minutes or their fourteen? Why listen forever to puppy-like song writers when one can hear and watch a great artist like Ella Shields? My third visit to Ella Shields convinces me that she is one of the finest artists I have ever heard, certainly as fine in her way as Guilbert and Chevalier were. It is a rare privilege to be able to enjoy artists like Grock—Mark Sheridan—who is now dead, I am told. Mark, with his "They all walk the wibbly-wobbly walk, they all wear the wibbly-wobbly ties," and so on.

ADVENTURES IN THE ARTS

Mark is certainly being missed by a great many
who care for the pleasure of the moment. When I
look at and listen to the aristocratic artist Ella
Shields, I feel a quality in her of the impeccable
Mrs. Fiske. And then I am thinking of another
great woman, Fay Templeton. What a pity we
must lose them either by death or by decisions in
life. Ella Shields with her charming typification
of "Burlington Bertie from Bow."

The other evening as I listened to Irene Franklin, I heard for certain what I had always thought
were notes from the magic voice of dear old Fay.
Unforgettable Fay. How can one ever say enough
about her? I think of Fay along with my single
glimpses of Duse, Ada Rehan, Coquelin. You see
how I love her, then. Irene Franklin has the quality of imitation of the great Fay without, I think,
the real magic. Nevertheless I enjoy her, and I
am certain she has never been finer than now. She
has enriched herself greatly by her experiences the
last two years, and seems at the height of her power.
It was good to get, once again, little glimpses of
her Childs waitress and the chambermaid. It
seemed to me that there was a richer quality of atmosphere in the little Jewish girl with the ring curls
and the red mittens, as also in her French girl with,
by the way, a beautiful gown of rich yellow silk
Frenchily trimmed in vermilion or orange, I couldn't
make out which. The amusing French girl, who
having picked up many fag-ends of English from

166

her experience with the *soldats Américains*—got her "animals" mixed—"you have my goat, I have your goat, et—tie ze bull outside," and so on. I am crossing Irene and Fay here because I think them similar, only I must say I think the magic was greater in Fay, because possibly Fay was the greater student of emotion. Fay had the undercurrent, and Irene has perfected the surface. If Irene did study Fay at any time, and I say this respectfully, she perhaps knows that Fay went many times to Paris to study Rejane. The light entertainer is, as we know, very often a person of real intellect.

If you want distinction, then, you will get it in the presence of Ella Shields. Her "Burlington Bertie" is nothing less than a chef d'œuvre; "Tom Lipton, he's got lots of 'oof—he sleeps on the roof, and I sleep in the room over him." Bertie, who, having been slapped on the back by the Prince of Wales (and some others) and asked why he didn't go and dine with "Mother," replied—"I can't, for I've just had a banana with Lady Diana. . . . I'm Burlington Bertie from Bow." Miss Shields shows also that she can sing a sentimental song without slushing it all over with saccharine. She has mastered the droll English quality of wit with real perfection. I regret I never saw Vesta Tilley, with whom the old tops compare her so favourably. Superb girls all these, Fay, Ella, Cissie, Vesta, as well as Marie Lloyd, and the other inimitable Vesta—Victoria.

Among the "coming soon," we have Miss Juliet, whom I recall with so much pleasure from the last immemorable Cohan Revue. I wait for her. I consider myself fortunate to be let in on James Watts. We thought our Eddy Foy a comic one. He was, for I remember the Gibson girl with the black velvet gown and the red flannel undershirt. I swing my swagger stick in the presence of Mr. Watts by way of applause. His art is very delicately understood and brought out. It has a fine quality of broad caricature with a real knowledge of economy such as Grock is master of. The three episodes are certainly funny enough. I find myself caring more for the first, called "June Day," since he reminds me so strongly in make-up of the French caricaturists in drawing, Rouveyre and Toulouse-Lautrec. Mr. Watts's feeling for satirical make-up is a fine shade of artistry in itself. He has excellent feeling for the broad contrast and for fierce insinuation at the same time. If you want real unalloyed fun, Mr. Watts will supply you. Nor will Grock disappoint you. Quite on the contrary, no matter what you are expecting.

I do not know why I think of vaudeville as I think of a collection of good drawings. Unless it is because the sense of form is the same in all of the arts. The acrobat certainly has line and mass to think of, even if that isn't his primal concern. He knows how he decorates the space on which he operates. To make another comparison, then, Grock is the Forain of vaudeville. He achieves great plastic beauty with distinguished economy of means. He dispenses with all superfluous gesture, as does the great French illustrator. Grock is entirely right about clownery. You are either funny or you are not. No amount of study will produce the gift for humour. It is there, or it isn't. Grock's gift for musicianship is a singular combination to find with the rest of his artistry. It goes with the remarkably refined look in his face, however, as he sits upon the back of the seatless chair, and plays the little concertina with superb execution. There are no "jumps" in Grock's performance. His moods flow from one into another with a masterly smoothness, and you are aware when he is finished that you have never seen that sort of foolery before. Not just that sort. It is the good mind that satisfies, as in the case of James Watts, and Miss Shields.

From elephants carrying in their trunks chatelaines of Shetland ponies, curtseying at the close of the charming act like a pretty miss at her first coming out, to such work as the Four Danubes give you as the closing number, with Irene as a lead, you are, to say the least, carried over the dreadful spots, such as the young man who sways out like a burlesque queen and tells you whom he was with before Keith got him. His name should be "Pusher," "Advance Man," or something of that sort, and not artist. What he gives you, you could find just as well if not better done on Fourteenth Street. He has a ribbon-counter, adenoid voice production that no really fine artist could afford. He will "get by," because anything does, apparently.

One turns to the big artist for relief, even though minor artists like The Brown Sisters charm so surely with their ivory and silver diamond-studded accordions, giving very pleasing transitions from grave to gay in arias and tunes we know. Accordions and concertinas are very beautiful to me, when played by artists like these girls, and by such as Joe Cawthorne, and Grock.

There are more dancing men of quality this season, it seems to me, who are obscured by dancing ladies of fame, and not such warrantable artistry. Perhaps it is because male anatomy allows of greater eccentricity and playfulness. There are no girls who have just such laughing legs as the inimitable Frances White. It is the long-legged American boy who beats the world in this sort of thing.

The lovely bit of hockey which James Barton gives is for me far more distinguished than all the rest of his work in the Winter Garden Revue. He is a real artist, but it is work that one sees rather a deal of this season, whereas the hockey dance is like nothing else to be found. A lovely moment of rhythmic leg work. We are now thoroughly familiar with the stage drunk, as we have long been familiarized by Weber and Fields with the stage Jew, which is fortunately passing out for lack of artist to present it. Leon Errol is good for once, even twice. He is quite alone in his very witty falls and runs. They are full of the struggle of the drunk to regain his character and manhood. The act lives on a very flat plane otherwise. It has no roundness.

I have come on my list to Mijares and Co., in "Monkey Business." We have the exquisite criterion always for the wire, in the perfect Bird Millman. "Monkey Business" is a very good act, and both men do excellent work on the taut and slack wire. "Monkey," in this case being a man, does as beautiful a piece of work as I know of. I have never seen a back somersault upon a high wire. I have never heard of it before. There may be whole generations of artists gifted in this particular stunt. You have here, nevertheless, a moment of very great beauty in the cleanness of this man's surprising agility and sureness. The monkey costume hinders the beauty of the thing. It should be done with pale blue silk tights against a cherry velvet drop, or else in deep ultramarine on an old gold background.

The acrobatic novelty called "The Legrohs" relies chiefly on its most exceptional member, who would be complete without the other two. He is most decidedly a virtuoso in vaudeville. Very gifted, certainly, if at moments a little disconcerting in the flexibility and the seemingly uncertain turns of his body. It is the old-fashioned contortionism saved by charming acrobatic variations. This "Legroh" knows how to make a superb pattern with his body, and the things he does with it are done with such ease and skill as to make you forget the actual physical effort and you are lost for the time being in the beauty of this muscular kaleidoscopic brilliancy. You feel it is like "puzzle—find the man" for a time, but then you follow his exquisite changes from one design into another with genuine delight, and appreciate his excessive grace and easy rapidity. He gives you chiefly the impression of a dragon-fly blown in the wind of a brisk morning over cool stretches of water. You would expect him to land on a lily-pad any moment and smooth his wings with his needle-like legs.

So it is the men and women of vaudeville transform themselves into lovely flower and animal forms, and the animals take on semblances of human sensibility in vaudeville. It is the superb arabesque of the beautiful human body that I care for most, and get the most from in these cameo-like bits of beauty and art. So brief they are, and like the wonders of sea gardens as you look through the glass bottoms of the little boats. So like the wonders of the microscopic, full of surprising novelties of colour and form. So like the kaleidoscope in the ever changing, ever shifting bits of colour reflecting each other, falling into new patterns with each twist of the toy. If you care for the iridescence of the moment you will trust vaudeville as you are not able to trust any other sort of a performance. You have no chance for the fatigue of problem. You

are at rest as far as thinking is concerned. It is
something for the eye first and last. It is something for the ear now and then, only very seldomly,
however. For me, they are the saviours of the dull-
est art in existence, the art of the stage. Duse was
quite right about it. The stage should be swept of
actors. It is not a place for imitation and photography. It is a place for the laughter of the
senses, for the laughter of the body. It is a place
for the tumbling blocks of the brain to fall in heaps.
I give first place to the acrobat and his associates
because it is the art where the human mind is for
once relieved of its stupidity. The acrobat is master of his body and he lets his brain go a-roving
upon other matters, if he has one. He is expected
to be silent. He would agree with William James,
transposing "music prevents thinking" into "talking
prevents silence." In so many instances, it prevents conversation. That is why I like tea chit-
chat. Words are never meant to mean anything
then. They are simply given legs and wings, and
they jump and fly. They land where they can, and
fall flat if they must. The audience that patronizes
vaudeville would do well to be present at most first
numbers, and remain for most or many of the closing ones. A number, I repeat, like the Four Danubes, should not be snubbed by any one.

I have seen recently, then, by way of summary,
four fine bits of artistry in vaudeville—Ella Shields,
James Watts, the Brothers Rath, and the Four Dan-

ubes. I shall speak again of these people. They are well worth it. They turn pastime into perfect memory. They are, therefore, among the great artists.

A CHARMING EQUESTRIENNE

I AM impelled to portray, at this time, my devotion to the little equestrienne, by the presence of a traveling circus in these lofty altitudes in which I am now living, seven thousand feet above the sea, in our great southwest. The mere sight of this master of the miniature ring, with all the atmosphere of the tent about him, after almost insurmountable difficulties crossing the mountains, over through the canyons of this expansive country, delivering an address in excellently chosen English, while poised at a considerable height on the wire, to the multitude on the ground below him, during which time he is to give what is known as the "free exhibit" as a high wire artist—all this turns me once more to the ever charming theme of acrobatics in general and equestrianism in particular, and it is of a special genius in this field that I wish to speak.

I have always been a lover of these artists of bodily vigour, of muscular melody, as I like to call it. As I watched this ringmaster of the little traveling circus, this master mountebank of the sturdy figure, ably poised upon his head on the high wire, outlined against the body of the high mountain in the near distance, about which the thunder clouds were huddling, and in and out of which the lightning was sharply playing, it all formed for me another of those perfect sensations from that phase of art expression known as the circus. My happiest memories in this field are from the streets of Paris before the war, the incomparably lovely fêtes. Only the sun knows where these dear artists may be now.

But I am wanting to tell of the little equestrienne, whose work has for the past five years been a source of genuine delight to me, charming little May Wirth, of Australian origin, with her lovely dark eyes, and captivating English accent. If you have a genuine sympathy for this sort of expression, it is but natural that you want to get inside the ring, and smell the turf with them, and so it was the representative of this gifted little woman who brought us together. It is, in the first place, a pity that there is so little written of the history of these people, so little material from which to gather the development of the idea of acrobatics in general, or of any one phase in particular. It would be impossible to learn who was the first aerial trapezist, for instance, or where high wire performing was brought from, just when the trick of adjusting the body to these difficult and strenuous rhythms was originated. They cannot tell you themselves. Only if there happens to be more than two generations in existence can you trace the development of this form of athletic entertainment. It may have begun with the Egyptians, it may have begun with the first gypsies.

176

A CHARMING EQUESTRIENNE

These people do not write their history, they simply make it among themselves, and it is handed down through the generations. When I asked May Wirth for information, she said she knew of none on the subject, save that she herself sprang from five generations of acrobats and equestrians, and that it is terrifically hard labour from beginning to end, equestrianism in particular, since it requires a knowledge of several if not all the other physical arts combined, such as high wire walking, handspring and somersault, trapeze work, bars, ballet dancing, etc.; that she herself had begun as a child, and had run the entire gamut of these requirements, coming out the finished product, so to speak, in all but ballet dancing, which she disliked, and wept always when the time came for her lesson in this department.

When one sees the incomparable brilliancy of this little woman of the horse, watching her marvellous ground work, which is in itself an example of virtuosity, one realizes what accomplishment alone can do, for she is not yet twenty-five, and the art is already in the condition of genius with her. Five handsome side-wheels round the ring, and a flying jump on the horse, then several complete somersaults on the horse's back while he is in movement round the ring, is not to be slighted for consideration, and if, as I have said, you have a love or even a fancy for this sort of entertainment, you all but worship the little lady for the thrill she gives you through this consummate mastery of hers.

"I always wanted to do what the boys could do, and I was never satisfied until I had accomplished it." This was the strongest assertion the little lady of the horse was moved to make while in conversation, and that the ring is more beautiful to work in than on a mat upon a stage, for it is in the ring that the horse is most at home, it is easier for him, and gives him greater muscular freedom, with the result naturally, that it is easier on the muscles of the human body while in action. I have never tired of this species of entertainment. It has always impressed me as being the most natural form of transposed physical culture, esthetically speaking. It does for the eye, if you are sensitive, what music does for the ear. It gives the body a chance to show its exquisite rhythmic beauty, as no other form of athletics can, for it is the beautiful plastic of the body, harmonically arranged for personal delight.

It is something for so young a woman to have walked away with first honours in her chosen field, yet like the true artist that she is, she is thinking always of how she can beautify her accomplishment to a still greater degree. She is mistress of a very difficult art, and yet the brilliancy of her performance makes it seem as if it were but the experiment of an afternoon, in the out-of-doors. Like all fine artists, she has brushed away from sight all aspects of labour, and presents you, with astounding ease, the apparent easiness of the thing. She is powerfully built, and her muscles are master of coordination, such as would be the envy of multitudes of men, and with all this power, she is as simple in her manner and appearance as is the young debutante at her coming out function. You are impressed with her sweetness and refinement, first of all, and the utter lack of show about her, as also with her brother who is a dapper young man of the very English type, who works with her, and acts as the dress-suited gentleman in this acrobatic ringplay of theirs. Three other members of her family take part also with her, the ring-mistress, a woman of possibly forty, acting as host, looking exceptionally well, handsome indeed, in grey and silver evening dress, with fine dark eyes and an older sister who opens the performance with some good work. This seems to me to be the modern touch, for there was a time when it was always the very well groomed ringmaster, with top hat and monocle, who acted as host of the ring.

It will likewise be remembered by those who saw the Hannafords at the circus, that they were also possessed of a very handsome ring-mistress, elegantly gowned, both of these older ladies lending great distinction, by their presence, to already brilliant performances. I would be very pleased to make myself historian for these fine artists, these esthetes of muscular melody. I should like very much to be spokesman for them, and point out to an enforcedly ignorant public, the beauties of this line of artistic expression, and to give historical ac-

count of the development of these various pictur-
esque athletic arts. Alas, that is not possible, for it
must remain forever in the limbo of tradition.

We shall have to be grateful beyond expression
for the beautiful art of May Wirth, and devote less
enthusiasm to asking of when and how it came about.
To have established one's art at the perfect point
in one's girlhood, is it not achievement, is it not
genius itself? Charming little May Wirth, first
equestrienne of the world, I congratulate you for
your beautiful presentation, for the excellence of its
technique, and for the grace and fascination contained therein. Triumph in youth, victory in the
heroic period of life, that surely is sufficient. Let
the bays fall upon her young head gleefully, for she
earned them with patience, devotion, intelligence,
and very hard labours. Salutations, little lady of
the white horse! How charming, how simple she
was, the little equestrienne as she rode away from
the door of the huge theatre, in her pale blue touring car. "I love the audiences here in this great
theatre, but O, I love the circus so much more!"
These were the sentiments of the little performer
as she rode away. She is now touring, performing
under the huge canvases in the open areas of the
middle West, and the little traveling circus is on
its way over the mountains. Fascinating people,
and a fascinating life for whom there is not, and
probably never will be, a written history; the story
of whose origin lies almost as buried as that of the

primitive peoples. Charming rovers, content with life near to the bright sky, charming people, for whom life is but one long day in which to make beautiful their bodies, and make joyful the eyes of those who love to look at them!

JOHN BARRYMORE IN PETER IBBETSON

THE vicissitudes of the young boy along the vague, precarious way, the longing to find the reality of the dream—the heart that knew him best— a study in sentimentality, the pathetic wanderings of a "little boy lost" in the dream of childhood, and the "little boy found" in the arms of his loved mother, with all those touches that are painful and all that are exquisite and poignant in their beauty —such is the picture presented by John Barrymore, as nearly perfect as any artist can be, in "Peter Ibbetson." Certainly it is as finished a creation in its sense of form, and of color, replete with a finesse of rare loveliness, as gratifying a performance, to my notion, as has been seen on our stage for many years. Perhaps if the author, recalling vain pasts, could realize the scum of saccharinity in which the play is utterly submerged, and that it struggles with great difficulty to survive the nesselrodelike sweetness with which it is surfeited, he would recognize the real distinction that Barrymore lends to a rôle so clogged by the honeyed sentimentality covering most of the scenes. Barrymore gives us that "quickened sense" of the life of the young man, a portrayal which takes the eye by "its fine edge of light," a portrayal clear and cool, elevated to a fine loftiness in his rendering.

The actor has accomplished this by means of a nice knowledge of what symbolic expression means to the art of the stage. He is certainly a painter of pictures and moods, the idea and his image perfectly commingled, endowing this mediocre play with true charm by the distinction he lends it, by sheer discretion, and by a power of selection. All this he brings to a play which, if it had been written nowadays, would certainly have convicted its author, and justly too, of having written to stimulate the lachrymal effusions of the shop-girl, a play about which she might telephone her girl friend, at which she might eat bon bons, and powder her nose again for the street. No artist, no accepted artist, has given a more suggestive rendering than has Barrymore here. It would be difficult to say where he is at his best, except that the first half of the play counts for most in point of strength and opportunity.

A tall frail young man, we find him, blanched with wonder and with awe at the perplexity of life, seeking a solution of things by means of the dream, as only the dreamer and the visionary can, lost from first to last, seemingly unloved in the ways boys think they want to be loved; that is, the shy longing boy, afraid of all things, and mostly of himself, in the period just this side of sex revelation. He is the neophyte—the homeless, pathetic Peter, perplexed with the strangeness of things real and temporal—vision and memory counting for all there is of reality to him, with life itself a thing as yet untasted. Who shall forget (who has a love for real expression) the entrance of Peter into the drawing-room of Mrs. Deane, the pale flowery wisp of a boy walking as it were into a garden of pungent spices and herbs, and of actions so alien to his own? We are given at this moment the keynote of mastery in delicate suggestion, which never fails throughout the play, tedious as it is, overdrawn on the side of symbolism and mystical insinuation.

One sits with difficulty through many of the moments, the literary quality of them is so wretched. They cloy the ear, and the mind that has been made sensitive, desiring something of a finer type of stimulation. Barrymore has evoked, so we may call it, a cold method—against a background of what could have been overheated acting or at least a super-abundance of physical attack—the warmth of the play's tender sentimentalities; yet he covers them with a still spiritual ardor which is their very essence, extracting all the delicate nuances and arranging them with a fine sense of proportion. It is as difficult an accomplishment for a man as one can imagine. For it is not given to many to act with this degree of whiteness, devoid of off colorings or alien tones. This performance of Barrymore in its spiritual richness, its elegance, finesse, and intelligence, has not been equaled for me since

JOHN BARRYMORE IN PETER IBBETSON

I saw the great geniuses Paul Orleneff and Eleonora Duse.

It is to be at once observed that here is a keen pictorial mind, a mind which visualizes perfectly for itself the chiaroscuro aspects of the emotion, as well as the spiritual, for Barrymore gives them with an almost unerring felicity, and rounds out the portrayal which in any other hands would suffer, but Barrymore has the special power to feel the value of reticence in all good art, the need for complete subjection of personal enthusiasm to the force of ideas. His art is akin to the art of silver-point, which, as is known, is an art of directness of touch, and final in the instant of execution, leaving no room whatever for accident or untoward excitement of nerve.

We shall wait long for the silver suggestiveness such as Barrymore gives us when Peter gets his first glimpse of Mary, Duchess of Towers. Who else could convey his realization of her beauty, and the quality of reminiscence that lingers about her, of the rapt amaze as he stands by the mantel-piece looking through the door into the space where he sees her in the midst of dancers under a crystal chandelier somewhere not very distant? Or the moment when he finds her bouquet neglected on the table in the drawing-room, with her lace shawl not far from his hands? Or when he finds himself alone, pressing his lips into the depth of the flowers as the curtain gives the finale to the scene with the whispered "l'amour"! These are moments of a real lyrist, and would match any line of Banville, of Ronsard, or of Austin Dobson for delicacy of touch and feeling, for freshness, and for the precise spiritual gesture, the "intonation" of action requisite to relieve the moments from what might otherwise revert to commonplace sentimentality.

Whatever the prejudice may be against all these emotions glacé with sugary frosting, we feel that his art has brought them into being with an unmistakable gift of refinement coupled with superb style. How an artist like Beardsley would have revelled in these moments is easy to conjecture. For here is the quintessence of intellectualized aquarelle, and these touches would surely have brought into being another "Pierrot of the Minute"—a new line drawing out of a period he knew and loved well. These touches would have been graced by the hand of that artist, or by another of equal delicacy of appreciation, Charles Conder—unforgettable spaces replete with the essence of fancy, of dream, of those farther recesses of the imagination.

Although technically and historically Barrymore has the advantage of excellent traditions, he nevertheless rests entirely upon his own achievements, separate and individual in his understanding of what constitutes plastic power in art. He has a peculiar and most sensitive temper, which can arrange points of relation in juxtaposition with a keen sense of form as well as of substance. He is, one might say, a masterly draftsman with a rich cool sense of color, whose work has something of the still force of a drawing of Ingres with, as well, the sensitive detail one finds in a Redon, like a beautiful drawing on stone. An excellent knowledge of dramatic contrasts is displayed by the brothers Barrymore, John and Lionel, in the murder scene, one of the finest we have seen for many years, technically even, splendid, and direct, concise in movement. Every superfluous gesture has been eliminated. From the moment of Peter's locking the door upon his uncle the scene is wrapped in the very coils of catastrophe, almost Euripedean in its inevitability. All of this episode is kept strictly within the realm of the imagination. It is an episode of hatred, of which there is sure to be at least one in the life of every young sensitive, when every boy wants, at any rate somewhere in his mind, to destroy some influence or other which is alien or hateful to him. The scene emphasizes once again the beauty of technical power for its own sake, the thrill of discarding all that is not immediately essential to simple and direct realization.

Little can be said of the play beyond this point, for it dwindles off into sentimental mystification which cannot be enjoyed by anyone under fifty, or appreciated by anyone under eighteen. It gives opportunity merely for settings and some rare moments of costuming, the lady with the battledore reminding one a deal of a good Manet. This and, of course, the splendid appearance of the Duchess of Towers in the first act—all these touches furnish more than a satisfying background for the very shy and frail Peter.

This performance of Barrymore holds for me the first and last requisite of organized conception in art —poise, clarity, and perfect suggestibility. Its intellectual soundness rules the emotional extravagance, giving form to what—for lack of form— so often perishes under an excess of energy, which the ignorant actor substitutes for the plastic element in all art. It has the attitude, this performance, almost of diffidence to one's subject-matter, except as the intellect judges clearly and coolly. Thus, in the sense of esthetic reality, are all aspects clarified and made real. From the outward inward, or from the inward outward, surface to depth or depth to surface—it is difficult to say which is the precise method of approach. John Barrymore has mastered the evasive subtlety therein, which makes him one of our greatest artists. The future will surely wait for his riper contributions, and we may think of him as one of our foremost artists, among the few, "one of a small band," as the great novelist once said of the great poet.

PART THREE

LA CLOSERIE DE LILAS

DIVINE Tuesday! I had wondered if those remarkable evenings of conversation in the rue de
Rome with Mallarmé as host, and Henri de Regnier
as guest, among many others, had been the inspira-
tion of the evenings at the Closerie de Lilas, where
I so often sat of an evening, watching the numbers
of esthetes gather, filling the entire café, rain or
shine, waiting unquestionably, for it pervaded the
air always, the feeling of suspense, of a dinner without host, of a wedding without bridegroom, in any
event waiting for the real genius of the evening, le
grand maitre prince de poètes, Paul Fort. The interesting book of Amy Lowell's, "Six French Poets,"
recalls these Tuesday evenings vividly to my mind,
and a number of episodes in connection with the idea
of poetry in Paris.

Poetry an event? A rather remarkable notion
it would seem, and yet this was always so, it was a
constituent of the day's passing, there was never a
part of the day in this arrondissement, when you
would not find here, there, everywhere, from the
Boul-Mich up, down Montparnasse to Lavenue's,
and back to the Closerie, groups of a few or of
many, obviously the artist or poet type, sometimes
very nattily dressed, often the reverse, but you found

them talking upon one theme, art, meaning either poetry or painting, cubistes, futuristes, orphistes and doubtless every "iste" in poetry from the symboliste period up to the "unanimistes" of the present time, or the then present time nearly two years before the war. It was a bit novel, even for a sensitive American, sitting there, realizing that it was all in the name of art, and for the heralding of genius—a kind of sublimated recruiting meeting for the enlistment in the army of expression of personality, or for the saving of the soul of poetry.

It was a spectacle, edifying in its purport, or even a little distressing if one had no belief in a sense of humour, for there were moments of absurdity about it as there is sure to be in a room filled with any type of concerted egotism. But you did not forget the raison d'etre of it all, you did not forget that when the "prince" arrived there was the spirit of true celebration about it, the celebration not only of an arrived artist, but of an idea close to the hearts and minds of those present, and you had a sense, too, of what it must have been like in that circle of, no doubt, a higher average of adherents, in the drawing room of the genius Mallarmé, who, from all accounts, was as perfected in the art of conversation, as he was in expression in art. When I read Miss Lowell's chapter on Henri de Regnier, I find myself before the door of the Mallarmé house in the rue de Rome, probably the only American guest, on that Sunday morning in June, just one given a privilege that could not mean as much as if I had been more conversant with the delicacies of the language.

It was the occasion of the placing of a tablet of homage to the great poet, at which ceremony Henri de Regnier himself was the chief speaker: a tall, very aristocratic, very elegant looking Frenchman, not any more to be called young, nor yet to be called old, but conspicuously simple, dignified, dressed in a manner of a gentleman of the first order, standing upon a chair, speaking, as one would imagine, with a flow of words which were the epitome of music itself to the ear. I had been invited by a poet well known in Paris, with several volumes to his credit and by a young literary woman, both of whom spoke English very creditably. After the ceremonies, which were very brief, and at which Madame Mallarmé herself was present, standing near the speaker, de Regnier, the entire company repaired to a restaurant near the Place Clichy, if I remember rightly. My hostess named for me the various guests as they appeared, Madame Rachilde, Reynaldo Hahn, André Gide, and a dozen other names less conspicuous, perhaps, excepting one, Léon Dierx, who was an old man, and whose death was announced about the city some days later. It was, needless to say, a conspicuous company and the dinner went off very quietly, allowing of course for the always feverish sound of the conversation of many people talking in a not very large room.

But all these suggestions recall for me once more
what such things mean to a people like the French,
or, let one say, Europeans as well. I wonder what
poetry or even painting will do, if they shall rise to
such a state in this country that we shall find our
masters of literature holding audience with this degree of interest like Fort, or as did all the great
masters of literature in Paris, hold forth in the name
of art, a divine Tuesday set apart for the admirable
worship of poetry, or of things esthetic. I can
imagine Amy Lowell doing something of this sort
after the custom of those masters she so admires,
with her seemingly quenchless enthusiasms for all
that is modern in poetry. I think we shall wait long
for that, for the time when we shall have our best
esthetics over the coffee, at the curbside under the
trees with the sun shining upon it, or the shadow of
the evening lending its sanction, under the magnetic
influence of such a one as Paul Fort or Francis
Jammes, or Emile Verhaeren—as it was once to be
had among such as Verlaine, Baudelaire and that
high company of distinguished painters who are now
famous among us.

The studio of Gertude Stein, that quiet yet always
lively place in the rue de Fleurus, is the only room
I have ever been in where this spirit was organized
to a similar degree, for here you had the sense of
the real importance of painting, as it used to be
thought of in the days of Pissarro, Manet, Degas,
and the others, and you had much, in all human ways,

LA CLOSERIE DE LILAS

out of an evening there, and, most of all, you had a fund of good humour thrust at you, and the conversation took on, not the quality of poetic prose spoken, as you had the quality of yourself and others, a kind of William James intimacy, which, as everyone knows, is style bringing the universe of ideas to your door in terms of your own sensations. There may have been a touch of all this at the once famed Brook Farm, but I fancy it was rather chill in its severity.

There is something of charm in the French idea of taking their discussions to the sunlight or the shadow under the stars, either within or outside the café, where you feel the passing of the world, and the poetry is of one piece with life itself, not the result of stuffy studios, and excessively ornate library corners, where books crowd out the quality of people and things. You felt that the café was the place for it, and if the acrobat came and sang, it was all of one fabric and it was as good for the poetry, as it was for the eye and the ear that absorbed it. Despite the different phases of the spectacle of Tuesday, at the Closerie de Lilas, you had the feeling of its splendour, its excellence, and, most of all, of its reality, its relationship to every other phase of life, and not of the hypersensitivity of the thing as we still consider it among ourselves in general; and if you heard the name of Paul Fort, or Francis Jammes, it was a definite issue in daily life, equal with the name of the great statesmen in importance, you were being introduced into a sphere of activities of the utmost importance, *that* poetry was something to be reckoned with.

It was not merely to hear oneself talk that artists like Mallarmé held forth with distinction, that artists like de Regnier and Fort devote themselves, however secretly, or however openly to the sacred theme. They had but one intention, and that to arrive at, and assist in the realization of the best state of poetry, that shall have carried the art further on its way logically, and in accordance with the principles which they have created for their time; endeavoring always to create fresh values, new points of contact with the prevailing as well as with the older outlines of the classics. It was, then, a spectacle, from our removed point of view, the gathering of the poetic multitude around the café tables, over the Dubonnet, the grenadines, and the café noir, of a Tuesday evening. It gave one a sense of perpetuity, of the indestructibility of art, in spite of the obstacles encountered in the run of the day, that the artist has the advantage over the layman in being qualified to set down, in shapes imperishable, those states of his imagination which are the shapes of life and of nature.

We may be grateful to Amy Lowell for having assembled for our consummation, in a world where poetry is not as yet the sublime issue as it was to be felt at every street corner, much of the spirit of the rue de Rome, the Café Novelles D'Athènes, and

LA CLOSERIE DE LILAS

the Closerie de Lilas, as well as the once famed corner of the Café D'Harcourt where the absinthe flowed so continuously, and from which some very exquisite poetry has emanated for all time. It is the first intimation we have of what our best English poetry has done for the best French poets of the present, and what our first free verse poet has done for the general liberation of emotions and for freedom of form in all countries. He has indicated the poets that are to follow him. He would be the first to sanction all this poetic discussive intensity at the curbside, the liberty and freedom of the café, the excellence of a divine Tuesday evening.

EMILY DICKINSON

IF I want to take up poetry in its most delightful and playful mood, I take up the verses of that remarkable girl of the sixties and seventies, Emily Dickinson, she who was writing her little worthless poetic nothings, or so she was wont to think of them, at a time when the now classical New England group was flourishing around Concord, when Hawthorne was burrowing into the soul of things, Thoreau was refusing to make more pencils and took to sounding lake bottoms and holding converse with all kinds of fish and other water life, and Emerson was standing high upon his pedestal preaching of compensations, of friendship, society and the oversoul, leaving a mighty impress upon his New England and the world at large as well.

I find when I take up Emily Dickinson, that I am sort of sunning myself in the discal radiance of a bright, vivid, and really new type of poet, for she is by no means worn of her freshness for us, she wears with one as would an old fashioned pearl set in gold and dark enamels. She offsets the smugness of the time in which she lived with her cheery impertinence, and startles the present with her uncommon gifts. Those who know the irresistible

EMILY DICKINSON

charm of this girl—who gave so charming a portrait of herself to the stranger friend who inquired for a photograph: "I had no portrait now, but am small like the wren, and my hair is bold like the chestnut burr, and my eyes like the sherry in the glass that the guest leaves," this written in July, 1862—shall be of course familiar with the undeniable originality of her personality, the grace and special beauty of her mind, charm unique in itself, not like any other genius then or now, or in the time before her, having perhaps a little of relationship to the crystal clearness of Crashaw, like Vaughan and Donne maybe, in respect of their lyrical fervour and moral earnestness, yet nevertheless appearing to us freshly with as separate a spirit in her verse creations as she herself was separated from the world around her by the amplitude of garden which was her universe. Emily Dickinson confronts you at once with an instinct for poetry, to be envied by the more ordinary and perhaps more finished poets. Ordinary she never was, common she never could have been, for she was first and last aristocrat in sensibility, rare and untouchable if you will, vague and mystical often enough, unapproachable and often distinctly aloof, as undoubtedly she herself was in her personal life. Those with a fondness for intimacy will find her, like all recluses, forbidding and difficult, if not altogether terrifying the mind with her vagueries and peculiarities.

Here was New England at its sharpest, brightest,

199

wittiest, most fantastic, most wilful, most devout, saint and imp sported in one, toying with the tricks of the Deity, taking them now with extreme profundity, then tossing them about like irresistible toys with an incomparable triviality. She has traced upon the page and with celestial indelibility that fine line from her soul which is like a fine prismatic light, separating one bright sphere from another, one planet from another planet, and the edge of separation is but faintly perceptible. She has left us this bright folio of her "lightning and fragrance in one," scintillant with stardust as perhaps no other before her, certainly not in this country, none with just her celestial attachedness, or must we call it detachedness, and withal also a sublime, impertinent playfulness which makes her images dance before one like offspring of the great round sun, fooling zealously with the universes at her feet, and just beyond her eye, with a loftiness of spirit and of exquisite trivialness seconded by none. Who has not read these flippant renderings, holding always some touch of austerity and gravity of mood, or the still more perfect "letters" to her friends, will, I think, have missed a new kind of poetic diversion, a new loveliness, evasive, alert, pronounced in every interval and serious, modestly so, and at a bound leaping as it were like some sky child pranking with the clouds, and the hills and the valleys beneath them, child as she surely was always, playing in some celestial garden space in her mind, where every species of tether was unendurable, where freedom for this childish sport was the one thing necessary to her ever young and incessantly capering mind—"hail to thee, blithe spirit, bird thou ever wert"!

It must be said in all justice, then, that "fascination was her element," everything to her was wondrous, sublimely magical, awsomely inspiring and thrilling. It was the event of many moons to have someone she liked say so much as good morning to her in human tongue, it was the event of every instant to have the flowers and birds call her by name, and hear the clouds exult at her approach. She was the brightest young sister of fancy, as she was the gifted young daughter of the ancient imagination. One feels everywhere in her verse and in her so splendid and stylish letters an unexcelled freshness, brightness of metaphor and of imagery, a gift of a peculiarity that could have come only from this part of our country, this part of the world, this very spot which has bred so many intellectual and spiritual entities wrapped in the garments of isolation, robed with questioning. Her genius is in this sense essentially local, as much the voice of the spirit of New England as it is possible for one to hold. If ever wanderer hitched vehicle to the comet's tail, it was the poetic, sprite woman, no one ever rode the sky and the earth as she did in this radiant and skybright mind of her.

She loved all things because all things were in one way or in another way bright for her, and of a blinding brightness from which she often had to hide her face. She embroidered all her thoughts with starry intricacies, and gave them the splendour of frosty traceries upon the windowpane in a frigid time, and of the raindrop in the sun, and summered them with fragrancing of the many early and late flowers of her own fanciful conjuring. They are glittering garlands of her clear, cool fancies, these poems, fraught in some instances, as are certain finely cut stones, with an exceptional mingling of lights coursing swiftly through them. She was avid of starlight and of sunlight alike, and of that light by which all things are illumined with a splendour not their own merely, but lent them by shafts from that radiant sphere which she leaned from, looking out gleefully upon them from the window of that high place in her mind.

To think of this poet is to think of crystal, for she lived in a radianced world of innumerable facets, and the common instances were chariots upon which to ride widely over the edges of infinity. She is alive for us now in those rare fancies of hers, with no other wish in them save as memorandum for her own eyes, and when they were finished to send them spinning across the wide garden, many of them to her favorite sister who lived far, far away, over beyond the hedge. You shall find in her all that is winsome, strange, fanciful, fantastic and irresistible in the eastern character and characteristic. She is first and best in lightsomeness of temper, for the eastern is known as essentially a tragic genius. She is perhaps the single exponent of modern times of the quality of true celestial frivolity. Scintillant was she then, and like dew she was and the soft summer rain, and the light upon the lips of flowers of which she loved to sing. Her mind and her spirit were one, soul and sense inseparable, little sister of Shelley certainly she was, and the more playful relative of Francis Thompson.

She had about her the imperishable quality that hovers about all things young and strong and beautiful, she was the sense of beauty ungovernable. What there are of tendencies religious and moral disturb in nowise those who love and have appreciation for true poetic essences. She had in her brain the inevitable buzzing of the bee in the belly of the bloom, she had in her eyes the climbing lances of the sun, she had in her heart love and pity for the innumerable pitiful and pitiable things. She was a quenchless mother in her gift for solace and she was lover to the immeasurable love. Like all aristocrats she hated mediocrity, and like all first rate jewels, she had no rift to hide. She was not a maker of poetry, she was a thinker of poetry. She was not a conjurer of words so much as a magician in sensibility. She has only to see and feel and hear to be in touch with all things with a name or with things that must be forever nameless. If she loved people, she loved them for what they were, if she despised them she despised them for what they did, or for lack of power to feel they could not do. Silence under a tree was a far more talkative experience with her than converse with one or a thousand dull minds. Her throng was the air, and her wings were the multitude of flying movements in her brain. She had only to think and she was amid numberless minarets and golden domes, she had only to think and the mountain cleft its shadow in her heart.

Emily Dickinson is in no sense toil for the mind accustomed to the labours of reading, she is too fanciful and delicious ever to make heavy the head, she sets you to laughter and draws a smile across your face for pity, and lets you loose again amid the measureless pleasing little humanities. I shall always want to read Emily Dickinson, for she points her finger at all tiresome scholasticism, and takes a chance with the universe about her and the first rate poetry it offers at every hand within the eye's easy glancing. She has made poetry memorable as a pastime for the mind, and sent the heavier ministerial tendencies flying to a speedy oblivion. What a child she was, child impertinent, with a heavenly rippling in her brain!

These random passages out of her writings will show at once the rarity of her tastes and the originality of her phrasing. "February passed like a kate, and I know March. Here is the light the stranger said was not on sea or land—myself could arrest it, but will not chagrin him"——

EMILY DICKINSON

"The wind blows gay today, and the jays bark like blue terriers."

"Friday I tasted life, it was a vast morsel. A circus passed the house — still I feel the red in my mind though the drums are out."

"The lawn is full of south and the odors tangle, and I hear today for the first the river in the tree."

> "The zeros taught us phosphorus
> We learned to like the fire
> By playing glaciers when a boy
> And tinder guessed by power
>
> Of opposite to balance odd
> If white a red must be!
> Paralysis, our primer dumb
> Unto vitality."

Then comes the "crowning extravaganza. . . . If I read a book, and it makes my whole body so cold no fire will ever warm me, I know that is poetry. If I feel physically as if the top of my head were taken off, I know that is poetry. Is there any other way? These are the only ways I know it."

No one but a New England yankee mind could concoct such humours and fascinatingly pert phrases as are found here. They are like the chatterings of the interrupted squirrel in the tree-hole at nut-time. There is so much of high gossip in these poetic turns of hers, and so, throughout her books, one finds a multitude of playful tricks for the pleased mind to run with. She was an intoxicated being, drunken with the little tipsy joys of the simplest form, shaped as they were to elude always her evasive imagination into thinking that nothing she could think or feel but was extraordinary and remarkable.

"Your letter gave no drunkenness because I tasted rum before—Domingo comes but once," etc., she wrote to Col. Higginson, a pretty conceit, surely to offer a loved friend. The passages offered will give the unfamiliar reader a taste of the sparkle of this poet's hurrying fancy and set her before the willing mind entrancingly, it seems to me. She will always delight those who find it in their way to love her elfish, evasive genius, and those who care for the vivid and living element in words will find her, to say the least, among the masters in her feeling for their strange shapes and the fresh significance contained in them. A born thinker of poetry, and in a great measure a gifted writer of it, refreshing many a heavy moment made dull with the weightiness of books, or of burdensome thinking. This poet-sprite sets scurrying all weariness of the brain, and they shall have an hour of sheer delight who invite poetic converse with Emily Dickinson. She will repay with funds of rich celestial coin from her rare and precious fancyings. She had that "oblique integrity" which she celebrates in one of her poems.

ADELAIDE CRAPSEY

ONE more satellite hurried away too soon! High
hints at least, of the young meteor finding its way
through space. Here was another of those, with
a vast fund of wishing in her brain, and the briefest
of hours in which to set them roaming. Brevities
that whirl through the mind as you read those cinquains of Adelaide Crapsey, like white birds through
the dark woodlands of the night. Cameos or cas-
tles, what is size? Is it not the same if they are of
one perfection of feeling? Such a little book of
Adelaide Crapsey, surely like cameos cut on shell,
so clear in outline, so rich in form, so brave in indications, so much of singing, so much of poetry,
of courage.

> "Just now,
> Out of the strange
> Still dusk—as strange, as still,
> A white moth flew; Why am I grown
> So cold?"

Isn't the evidence sufficient here of first rate poetic gifts, sensibility of an exceptional order? Contrast in so many ways with that perhaps more radiant and certainly more whimsical girl, with her rarest of flavours, she with her "whip of diamond, riding to meet the Earl"! I think geniuses like Keats

or Shelley would have said "how do you do, poet?"
to Adelaide Crapsey and her verse, lamenting also
that she flew over the rainbowed edge of the dusk
too soon, like the very moth over the garden wall,
early in the evening. It is sure that had this poet
been allowed her full quota of days, she would have
left some handsome folios bright enough for any
one caring for verse at its purest. Pity there was
not time for another book at least, of her verses, to
verify the great distinction conferred. She might
have walked still more largely away with the
wreaths of recognition. Not time for more books,
instead of so much eternity at her bedside. She
would surely have sent more words singing to their
high places and have impressed the abundant out-
put of the day with its superficiality by her seriousness. There is no trifling in these poetic things of
hers. Trivial might some say who hanker after
giantesque composition. Fragile are they only in
the sense of size, only in this way are they small.

Those who know the difficulties of writing poetic
composition are aware of the task involved in creating such packed brevities. Emily Dickinson
knew this power. "H. D." is another woman who
understands the beauty of compactness. Superb
sense of economy, of terseness the art calls for, excessive pruning and clipping. Singular that these
three artists, so gifted in brevity were women.
There is little, after all, in existence that warrants
lengthy dissertation. Life itself is epigrammatic and

brief enough. No volumes needed by way of explanation. The fascinating enigma diverts and perplexes everyone alike. The simple understand it best, or at least they seem to do so. Segregation, aloofness, spiritual imprisonment, which is another name for introspection, the looking out from bars of the caged house, all this discovers something through penetration. Walking with life is most natural, grazing its warm shoulder. There is little room for inquiry if one have the real feeling of life itself. Poetry is that which gleans most by keeping nearest to life. Books and firesides avail but little. Secretaries for the baggage of erudition do not enhance poetic values, they encumber them. Poetry is not declamation, it is not propaganda, it is breathing natural breaths. There is nothing mechanical about poetry excepting the affectation of forms. Poetry is the world's, it is everybody's. You count poetry by its essence, and no amount of studied effect, or bulging erudition will create that which is necessary, that which makes poetry what it is. The one essential is power to sing, and the intelligence to get it down with degrees of mastery or naturalness, which is one and the same thing.

Real singing is unusual as real singers are rare. Adelaide Crapsey shows that she was a real singer, essentially poet, excellent among those of our time. She impresses her uncommon qualities upon you, in the cinquains of hers, with genuinely incisive force. She has so much of definiteness, so much of technical beauty, economy, all very valuable assets for a true poet. She had never been touched with the mania for journalistic profusion. She cared too much for language to ride it. She cared too much for words to want to whip them into slavery. She was outside of them, looking on, as it might be, through crystal, at their freshness. She did not take them for granted. They were new to her and she wanted the proper familiarity. She worked upon a spiritual geometric all her own. She did not run to the dictionary for eccentricities, she did not hunt words out of countenance. They were natural to her. She wanted most their simple beauty, and she succeeded. She had dignity, a rare gift in these times. She raises herself above the many by her fine feeling for the precision. That is her artistry, the word, the thing of beauty and the joy forever with her.

It is to be regretted that Adelaide Crapsey had no more time for the miniature microscopic equations, the little thing seen large, the large thing seen vividly. She might have spent more hours with them and less with her so persistent guest, this second self at her side; ironic presence, when she most would have strode with the brighter companion, her first and natural choice. Her contribution is conspicuous among us for its balance and its intellectualism tempered with fine emotions. She had so much to settle for herself, so much bargaining for the little escapes in which to register herself consistently, so much of consultation for her body's sake, that her mind flew the dark spaces about her bed with consistent feverishness.

Reckoning is not the genius of life. It is the painful, residual element of reflection. One must give, one must pay. It is not inspiring to beg for breath, yet this has come to many a fine artist, many a fine soul whose genius was far more of the ability for living, with so little of the ability for dying. You cannot think along with clarity, with the doom of dark recognition nudging your shoulder every instant. There must be somehow apertures of peace for production. Adelaide Crapsey's chief visitant was doom. She saw the days vanishing, and the inevitable years lengthening over her. No wonder she could write brevities, she whose existence was brevity itself. The very flicker of the lamp was among the last events. What, then, was the fluttering of the moth but a monstrous intimation. If her work was chilled with severity, it was because she herself was covered with the cool branches of decision. Nature was cold with her, hence there is the ring of ice in these little pieces of hers. They are veiled with the grey of many a sunless morning.

> "These be
> Three silent things;
> The falling snow,—the hour
> Before the dawn,—the mouth of one
> Just dead."

Here you have the intensity once more of Adelaide Crapsey. It haunts you like the something on the dark stairway as you pass, just as when, on the roadway in the dead of night, the twig grazing one's cheek would seem like the springing panther at one's throat. Dramatic vividness is certainly her chief distinction. No playfulness here, but a stout reckoning with austere beauty. The wish to record the element at its best that played so fierce a rôle in her life. She writes her own death hymn, lays her own shroud out, spaces her own epilogue as if to give the engraver, who sets white words on white stone, the clue, stones the years stare on, leaving the sunlight to streak the old pathos there, and then settles herself to the long way of lying, to the sure sleep that glassed her keen eyes, shutting them down too soon on a world that held so much poetry for her.

The titles of her cinquains, such as "November night", "The guarded wound", "The warning", "Fate defied", and the final touch of inevitability in "The Lonely Death", so full of the intensity of last moments, intimate the resolute presence of the grey companion of the covering mists. It must be said hurriedly that Adelaide Crapsey was not all doom. By no means. The longer pieces in her tiny book attest to her feeling for riches, and the lyrical wonders of the hour. Her fervour is the artist's fervour, the longing, coming really to passion, to hold and fix forever the shapes that were loveliest to her.

ADELAIDE CRAPSEY

That is the poet's existence, that is the poet's labour, and his last distress. No one wants to give in to a commonplace world when the light that falls on it is lovelier than the place it falls on. If you cannot transpose the object, transport it, however simply, however ornately, then of what use is poetry? It is transport!

Adelaide Crapsey was efficient in her knowledge of what poetry is, as she was certainly proficient as workman. She was lapidary more than painter or sculptor. It was a beautiful cutting away, and a sweeping aside of the rifts and flaws. That is to say, she wanted that. She wanted the white light of the perfect gem, and she could not have been content with just matrix, with here and there embedded chips. She was a washer of gold, and spared no labours for the bright nuggets she might get, and the percentage of her panning was high. But the cloud hung on the mountain she clomb, and her way was dimmed.

> "In the cold I will rise, I will bathe
> In the waters of ice; Myself
> Will shiver, and will shrive myself
> Alone in the dawn, and anoint
> Forehead and feet and hands;
> I will shutter the windows from light,
> I will place in their sockets the four
> Tall candles and set them a-flame
> In the grey of the dawn; And myself
> Will lay myself straight in my bed,
> And draw the sheet under my chin."

There could be no more of resolute finality in this chill epilogue. There is the cold of a thousand years shuddering out of this scene, it is the passing, the last of this delicate and gifted poet, Adelaide Crapsey. If she has written more than her book prints, these must surely be of her best. She took the shape of that which she made so visible, so cold, so beautiful. With her white wings she has skirted the edge of the dusk with an incredible calm. No whimpering here. Too much artistry for that; too much of eye to let heart rule. The gifts of Adelaide Crapsey were high ones, and that she left so little of song is regrettable, even though she left us a legacy of some of the best singing of the day. It is enough to call her poet, for she was among the first of this hour and time. She had no affectations, no fashionable theories and ambitions. She simply wrote excellent verse. That is her beautiful gift to us.

FRANCIS THOMPSON

If ever a meteor fell to earth it was Francis Thompson. If ever a star ascended to that high place in the sky where sit the loftier planets in pleasant company, it was this splendid poet. Stalking through the shadows of the Thames Embankment to find his clear place in the milky way, is hardly the easiest road for so exceptional a celebrity. It is but another instance of the odd tradition perpetuating itself, that some geniuses must creep hand and knee through mire, heart pierced with the bramble of experience, up over the jagged pathways to that still place where skies are clear at last. Thompson is the last among the great ones to have known the dire vicissitude, direst, if legends are true, that can befall a human being. We have the silence of his saviour friends, the Meynells, saying so much more than their few public words, tender but so careful. What they knew, and what the walls of the monastery of Storrington must have heard in that so pained stillness, there, is probably beyond repetition for pathos. De Quincey had taught him much in the knowledge of hardship. Whether it is just similarity of experience or a kind of imitation in nature, is not easy to say. It was hardly the example to repeat. It is singular enough also, that De Quin-

215

cey's "Ann" should have become so vivid a repetition to Thompson, in just the same terms.

London has no feeling for the peace of poets. They are the little things in the confused maelstrom of human endeavor. Poets are taught with the whip. They must bleed for their divine idea, or so it was then. Sometimes it seems as if a change had come, for so many poets sit in chairs of ease these days. Science produces other kinds of discomfort, and covers the old misery with a new tapestry of contrasts. I doubt if many poets are selling matches these days, living on eleven pence a day. There is still the poet who knows his cheap lodging. There seems enough of them still for high minds to crawl into, and yet there is another face to the misery.

Thompson was seraph from the first. You see the very doom burning out of his boy's eyes in the youthful portrait, and you see the logical end in that desperate and pitiful mask, the drawing of the last period in the Meynell Book. His was certainly the severed head, and his feet were pathetically far away, down on a stony earth. That he should have forfeited the ordinary ways of ease, is as consistent with his appearance, as it was necessary to his nature. That he should find himself on the long march past the stations of the cross, to the very tree itself, for his poetic purpose, if it is in keeping with tradition, is not precisely the most inspiring aspect of human experiences. Human he was not, as we like to think

of human, for he was too early in his career marked
for martyr. There is the note of cricket-time in
his earlier life, and how long this attached to the
physical delights of his being cannot be told here.
His eyes were lodged too far in heaven to have
kept the delights for long, to have comprehended all
that clogged his impatiently mercurial feet.

"The abashless inquisition of each star" was the
scrutiny that obsessed his ways, the impertinence
that he suffered most; for he had the magnitude of
soul that hungered for placement, and the plague
of two masters was on him. Huntress and "Hound"
he had to choose between, beauty and the insatiable
Prince; harsh and determined lovers, both of
them, too much craving altogether for an artistic
nature. The earth had no room for him and he
did not want heaven so soon. He was not saint,
even though his name followed him even, for recognition.

"Stood bound and helplessly, for Time to shoot
his barbed minutes at me, suffered the trampling
hoof of every hour," etc., all this confided to some
childish innocent in "The child's kiss". Whom else
should he tell but a child? Where is the man or
woman with understanding but has the "child"
lodged somewhere for sympathy, for recognition?
The clearest listener he could find, and the least
commiserative, happily. "The heart of childhood,
so divine for me", is but typical of a being so
dragged, and emaciate with the tortures of the body,

in earth places where no soul like his could ever be at home. What was Preston, or Ashton-under-Lyne to him, more than Kensall Green is to him now? What is such dust in his sky but some blinding and blowing thing? What is there for singer to do but sing until the throat cracks? Even the larks and the thrushes do that. They end their morning and evening with a song. He was brother to these birds in that loftiness. He sang, and sang, and sang, while flesh fainted from hunger and weakness.

Had not Storrington come to him in the dark places of London, we should have had no "Hound of Heaven", and without that masterpiece what would modern poetry do? He sang to cover up his wounds with climbing music. That was his sense of beauty. He filled his hollowing cheek with finer things than moaning. He might have wept, but they were words instead of drops.

It will be difficult to find loftier song as to essences. We shall have room for criticising stylistic extravagances, archaisms of a not interesting order for us, yet there will be nothing said but the highest in praise of his genius. Excess of praise may be heaped upon him without cessation, and it may end in the few cool yet incisive words that fell from the lips of Meredith, with the violets from another's worshipped hands, "a true poet, one of a small band." Poets of this time will have much to gather from Thompson in point of sincerity. There is terrific

mastery of words, which is like Shakespeare in felicity we do not encounter so often it seems to me.

Thompson has scaled the white rainbow of the
night, and sits in radiant company among the first
planetary strummers of song. His diamond is pure,
and the matrix that hid him so long from showing
his glinted facets is chipped away of miseries carried
down with death. They will soon be forgotten by
the multitude as death itself made him forget them.
We have his chants and his anthems and plainsongs
to remind us of the one essential, of how lofty a
singer passed down our highroad. "Dusty with
tumbling about amid the stars!" That is what he
is for us now, if he rolled in too much clay of earth.
Shelley might have turned his own handsome phrase
on him, for they both strode the morning of their
bright minds like sun the sky, with much of the same
solemn yet speedy gait. There are times when they
are certainly of the one radiance, lyrical and poetical.
Their consuming intellectual interests were vastly
apart, as were their paths of spirit.

I think we shall have no more "dread of height".
Poetry has passed into scientific discovery. Intellectual passions are the vogue, earth is coming into
its own, for there is no more heaven in the mind.
We are showing our humanities now, and the soul
must wait a little, and remain speechless in some
dull corner of the universe. Thompson was the last
to believe. We are learning to think now, so poetry

has come to calculation. Rhapsody and passion are romantic, and we are not romantic. The last Rhapsodist was Francis Thompson, and in the sense of lyrical fervour, the last great poet was Francis Thompson.

ERNEST DOWSON

It is late to be telling of Dowson, with the eighteen-nineties nearly out of sight, and yet it is Dowson and Lionel Johnson that I know most of, from the last of this period. Poles apart these two poets are, the one so austere and almost collegiate in adherence to convention, the other too warm to let a coldness obsess his singing. There doesn't seem to be anything wonderful about Dowson, and yet you want to be saying a line of his every now and then, of him "that lived, and sang, and had a beating heart," ere he grew old, and he grew old so soon. "Worn out by what was really never life to him," is a prefatorial phrase I recall. There was a genuine music in Dowson, even if it was smothered in lilies and roses and. wine of the now old way of saying things. "Come hither child, and rest—Behold the weary west," might have been the thing he was saying to himself, so much is this the essence of his lost cause.

There is a languor and a lack of power to lift a hand toward the light, too much a trusting of the shadow. "I have flung roses, roses riotously with the throng, to put those pale lost lilies out of mind." Always verging on a poetic feeling not just like ourselves in these days, and yet Dowson was a poet. He caressed words until they sang for him the one plaint that he asked of them. That he was obsessed of the beauties and the intimations of Versailles, is seen in everything he did, or at least he imbibed this from Verlaine. He was himself a pale wanderer down soft green allées, he had a twilight mind struggling toward the sun, which was too bright for him, for the moon was his brightest light. Echoes of Verlaine linger through his verse and a strain of Poe is present, poet whom he with his French taste admired so much, two very typical idols for a young man with a sentimental journey to pursue. Lost Adelaides, to keep him steeped in the sorrow that he cherished, for he petted his miseries considerably; or was it that he was most at home when he was unhappy? He would rather have seen the light of day from a not quite clear window, for instead of a clear hill, he might see a vague castle of his fancy somewhere. He hadn't the sweep of a great poet, and yet somehow there was the linnet in him, there was the strain of the lute among the leaves, there was the rustle of a soft dress audible, and the passing of hands he could not ever hold.

He was the poet of the lost treasure. "Studies in Sentiment" is, I think, the title of a small book of prose of his. He might have called his poems "Studies in sentimentality". And yet, for his time, how virile and vigorous he sounds beside "Posies out of Rings", of his friend Theodore Peters, of the renaissance cloak, the cherry coloured velvet cloak embroidered in green leaves and silver veinings, so full of the sky radiance of Dowson himself, this cloak. Cherry sounds red and passionate. But it was a cherry of olden time, with the bloom quite gone, the dust of the years permeating its silken warp. It reposes here in America, the property of an artist of that period.

One likes Dowson because of his sincerity, and a clear beauty which, if not exactly startling, was in its way truly genuine. It was merely too late for Dowson, and it was probably too soon. Swinburne had strummed the skies with every kind of song, and Verlaine had whispered every secret of the senses there was, in the land of illusion and vaguery. Dowson was worshipper of them both, for it was sound first and last that he cared most for, the musical mastery of the one and the sentimentality of the other. He was far nearer Verlaine in type. He had but the one thing to tell of, and that was lost love, and he told it over and over in his book of verse. His Pierrot of the Minute was himself, and his Cynara was the ever vanishing vision of his own insecurity and incapability. He perished for the love of hands. He is so like someone one knows, whom one wants to talk to tenderly, touch in a friendly way, and say as little as possible. He comes to one humanly first, and asks you for your eye to his verse afterward, something of the "Little boy

Lost", in his so ineffectual face, weak with sweetness and hidden in shyness, covered with irresponsibility, or lack of power to be responsible.

He was a helpless one, that is certain. He resorted to the old-fashioned methods of the decadents for maintaining the certain requisite melancholy apparently necessary to sing a certain way. In the struggle of that period, he must have seemed like a very clear, though a very sad singer. There were no lilies or orchids in his buttonhole, and no strange jewels on his fingers, for you remember, it was the time of "Monsieur Phocas", and the art of Gustave Moreau. He was plain and sincere, and pathetic, old-fashioned too in that he was bohemian, or at least had acquired bohemianism, for I think no Englishman was ever really bohemian. Dieppe and the docks had gotten him, and took away the sense of mastery over things that a real poet of power must somehow have. He was essentially a giver-in. His neurasthenia was probably the reason for that. It was the age of absinthe and little taverns, for there was Verlaine and the inimitable Café d'Harcourt, which, as you saw it just before the war, had the very something that kept the Master at his drinks all day.

Murger, Rimbaud, Verlaine had done the thing which has lasted so singularly until now, for there are still echoes of this in the air, even to the present day. Barmaids are memories, and roseleaves dried and set in urns, for that matter, too. How far away it all seems, and they were the substance of poetry then. Sounds were the important things for Dowson, which is essentially the Swinburne echo. Significant then, that he worshipped "the viol, the violet, and the vine" of Poe. There was little else but. singing in his verse however. His love of Horace did less for him than the masters of sound, excepting that the vision comes in the name "Cynara". But it was all struggle for Dowson, a battle with the pale lily. It was for this he clung to cabmen's lounging places. He was looking for places to be out of the play in. He couldn't have survived for long, and yet there is a strain of genuine loveliness, the note of pure beauty in the verse of Dowson. He was poet, and kept to his creed with lover-like tenacity.

He helped close a period that was distinguished all over the world, the period of the sunflower. Apart from its wildest and most spectacular genius, it has produced Lionel Johnson with his religious purity, and Aubrey Beardsley. It was the time of sad and delicate young men. They all died in boyhood really. These were, I think, with Dowson the best it offered. We never read Arthur Symons for his power in verse, he with so much of the rose-tinted afterglow in him, so much of the old feeling for stage doors and roses thrown from the boxes, and the dying scent of lingerie. His essays will be a far finer source of delight for a much longer time, for therein is the best poetry he had to offer.

Dowson was, let us say not mockingly, the boyish whimperer in song. He was ineffectual, too much so, to take up the game of laughter for long. That would have been too strenuous for him, so he had to sit and weep tears of wordy rain. "Il pleut dans mon cœur" was the famous touch of his master, it was the loudest strain in him. That was the lover-strain, and Dowson was the lover dying of love, imaginary love probably, and saw everywhere something to remind him of what he had pathetically lost. If there had been a little savage in him, he would have walked away with what he wanted. He maybe did have a try or two, but they couldn't have endured, for he wasn't loving a particular Adelaide. That was the name he gave to love, for it was woman's lips, and eyes and hands that he cared most for, or at least seemed most to care.

It was in the vision that crossed his ways in the dark and boisterous taverns where love finds strange ways for expression, that the singleness of feeling possessed him. It was among the rougher elements of dock life that his refinements found their level. Dowson sang and sang and sang, until he grew old at thirty-three, "worn out by what was never really life to him". Aged pierrot, gone home to his mother, the Moon, to bask forever in the twilight of his old and vague fancies. There might he strum his heart out in the old way, and the world would never hear, for it has lost the ear for this kind of song. Perhaps in two hundred years, in other

226

"golden treasuries" there may appear the songs of Dowson as among the best of those early and late singers of the nineteenth century. We cannot say now, for it cloys a little with sweets for us at this time, though it was then the time of honey and jasmine, and the scent of far away flowers. Pierrot of the glass, with the hours dripping away in fine, gold rain. That was the genius of poets like Dowson, and pierrot was the master of them all.

HENRY JAMES ON RUPERT BROOKE

HENRY JAMES on Rupert Brooke! Here is certainly a very wide interval, separated, artist and subject, by the greatest divergence of power, and one may be even amazed at the contrast involved. He is surely, James, in all his elaborateness, trying to square the rose and compute the lily, algebraical advances upon a most simple thesis. Brooke—a nature so obvious, which had no measure at all for what the sum had done to him, and for all that about him, or for those stellar ecstasies which held him bound with fervour as poet, planetary swimmer, and gifted as well with a fine stroke for the sea, and runner of all the beautiful earth places about the great seas' edge.

For me, there is heaviness and over-elaboration paramount in this preface to the Letters from America, excess of byword, a strained relationship with his subject, but that would of course be Jamesian, and very naturally, too. It is hardly, this preface, the tribute of the wise telling of beautiful and "blinding youth", surely more the treatise of the problemist forging his problem, as the sculptor might; something too much of metal or stone, too ponderous, too severe let one say, for its so gracing and brightening theme, something not springing into bloom, as does the person and personality of the young subject himself. Only upon occasion does he really come upon the young man, actual, forgetful of all but him.

There is no question, if the word of those be true who had relation however slight or intimate with Brooke, that he was an engrossing theme, and for more than one greater than himself, as certainly he was for many much less significant than James. It is distinguished from the young poet's point of view that he was impressed, and that as person to person he really did see him in a convincing manner, as might one artist of great repute find himself uncommonly affected by the young and so living poet with more than a common gift for creation. It seems to me however that James is not over certain as to how poetic all things are in substance, yet all the while treating Brooke coolly and spaciously as an artist should.

I did not know Brooke, and I know nothing of him beyond various photos showing him one way, quite manly and robust, and I feel sure he was so, and in another way as neither youth nor man, but something idyllic, separate and seraph-like, untouched mostly with earthly experience. These pictures do show that he was, unquestionably, a bright gust of England, with an almost audible splendour about even these poor replicas, which make it seem that he did perform the ascribed miracle, that England really had brought forth of her brightest and best, only to lay away her golden fruitage in dust upon the borders of a far and classical sea, with an acute untimeliness. But respectfully let me say, I think much in these hours of the incongruity and pathos of excessive celebration. There shall not be for long, singers enough to sing high songs commensurate with the delights of those numberless ones "who lived, and sang, and had a beating heart", those who have sped into the twilight too soon, having but a brief time to discover if years had bright secrets for them or clear perspective. There shall always lack the requisite word for them who have made many a dull morning splendid with faith, they who have been the human indication immeasurably of the sun's rising, and of the truth that vision is a thing of reason.

Of Brooke and the other dead poets as well, there has, it seems to me, been too much of celebration. But of Brooke and his poetry, which is a far superior product to these really most ordinary "Letters", there is in these poetic pieces too much of what I want to call "University Cleavage", an excess of old school painting, too much usage of the warm image, which, though emotional, is not sensuous enough to express the real poetic sensuousness, to make the line or the word burn passionately, too much of the shades of Swinburne still upon the horizon. Rose and violet of the eighteen ninety hues have for long been dispensed with, as has the pierrot and his moon. We have in this time come to like hardier colourings, which are for us more satisfying, and more poetic. We hardly dare use the hot words of "Anactoria" in our day. To be sure rose is English, for it has been for long a very predominant shade on the young face of England, but in Brooke there is an old age to the fervour, and in spite of the brilliant youth of the poet, there is an old age in the substance and really in the treatment as well. We are wanting a fresher intonation to those images, and expect a new approach, and a newer aspect. It is not to adhere by means of criticism to the prevailing graveyard tendency, nor do we want so much of the easy and cheap journalistic element, as comes so often in the so named "free verse". What is really wanted is an individual consistency, and a brightness of imagery which shall be the poet's own by reason of his own personal attachment, and not simply the variance of the many-in-one poetry of the day.

It is not enough to write passably, it is only enough when there are several, or even one, who will give their or his own peculiar contact with those agencies of the day, the hour, and the moment, who will find or invent a style best suited to themselves. Attempts at excessive individualism will never create true individualistic expression, no affected surprise in personal perversity of image or metaphor will make a real poet, or real poetry. There must be first and last of all, a sure ardour, the poet's very own, which will of itself support obvious, or even slightly detectable, influences. It is not enough to declaim oneself, or propose continually one's group. The single utterance is what is necessary, a real freshness of vocalization which is, so to speak, the singer's own throat. If he be original in his freshness, we shall be able to single him away from the sweeping movements of the hour by his very "specialness" in touch, that pressure of the mind and spirit upon the page, which is his.

We shall translate a poet through his indications and intentions as well as through his arrivals, and we must condemn no one to fame beyond his capacity or deserts. We have never the need of extravagant laud. It is not enough to praise a poet for his personal charm, his beauty of body and of mind and soul, for these are but beautiful things at home in a beautiful house. In the case of Brooke, we have ringing up among hosts of others, James's voice that he was all of this, but I would not wish to think it was the wish of any real poet to be "condemned to sociability", merely because he was an eminently social being, or because he was the exceptionally handsome, among the many less so; or be condemned to overpraise for what is after all but an indication to poetic power. "If I should die", is of course a very lovely sonnet, and it is the true indication of what Brooke might have been, but it is not the reason to be doomed to find all things wonderful in him. For in the state of perfection, if one see always with a lancet eye, we really do accentuate the essence of beauty by a careful and very direct critical sense, which can and should, when honorably exercised, show up delicately, the sense of proportion.

HENRY JAMES ON RUPERT BROOKE

It is as much a part of the artist's equipment to find fault as it is to praise, for he wants by nature the true value with which he may relate himself to the sense of beauty. It seems, perhaps only to me, that in Brooke's poems there is but a vigorous indication to poetic expression, whereas doubtless the man himself was being excessively poetic, hour and moment together, and spent much energy of mind and body poetizing sensation. For me, there is a journalistic quality of phrasing and only very rarely the unusual image. As for the "Letters", they are loose and jotty in form, without distinction either in observation or in form, without real felicity or uniqueness. Art is nothing if it is not the object, or the idea, or experience seen in review, with clarity. In Brooke, I feel the super-abundance of joy in the attractiveness of the world, but I do not feel the language of him commensurate or distinguished in the qualities of poetic or literary art. There seems to me to be too much of the blown lock and the wistful glance, too much of the attitudinized poet, lacking, I may even say, in true refinement, often.

A too comfortable poet, and poetry of too much verve without incision, too much "gesturing", which is an easy thing for many talented people, and there is also missing for me the real grip of amazement. You will not find anything in the letters that could not have been done by the cub reporter, save possibly in the more charming of the letters with reference to swimming in the South Seas. Here you feel Brooke at home instantly, and the picturing is natural and easy. But other than this, you will find no phrasing to compare with passages of James's preface, such, for instance, as the "sky-clamour of more dollars", surely a vastly more incisive phrase regarding the frenzies of New York, than all that Brooke essays to tell of it. Brooke is distinctly "not there" too often in these so irregular letters of his. Letters are notably rare in these times anyhow, and so it is with the letters of Brooke. We look for distinction, and it is not to be found, they have but little of the intimacy with their subjects that one expects.

As to his poetry, it seems to be a poetry rapidly approaching state approval, there is in it the flavour of the budding laureate, it seems to me to be poetry already "in orders". Brooke was certainly in danger of becoming a good poet, like the several other poets who perished in the throes of heroism. Like them, he would, had he lived, have had to save himself from the evils of prosperity, poetically speaking. He would have had to overcome his tendency toward what I want to call the old-fashioned "gold and velvet" of his words, a very definite haze hanging over them of the ill effect of the eighteen-ninety school, which produced a little excellent poetry and a lot of very tame production. Poetry is like all art, difficult even in its freest interval. Brooke must rest his claim to early distinction perhaps upon the "If I should die" sonnet alone, he would certainly have had to come up considerably, to have held the place his too numerous personal admirers were wont to thrust upon him. Unless one be the veritable genius, sudden laurels wither on the stem with too much of morning.

This poet had no chance to prove what poetry of his would have endured the long day, and most of all he needed to be removed from too much love of everything. The best art cannot endure such promiscuity, not an art of specific individual worth. In the book which is called "Letters from America", the attraction lies in its preface, despite the so noticeable irrelevancy of style. It seems to me that James might for once have condescended to an equal footing with his theme, for the sake of the devoutness of his intention, and have come to us for the moment, the man talking of the youth. He might then have told us something really intimate of "Rupert", as he so frequently names him, for this would indicate some intimacy surely, unless perchance he was "Rupert" to the innumerables whom he met, and who were sure of his intimacy on the instant's introduction, which would indeed be "condemned to sociability".

This book is in two pieces, preface and content, and we are conscious chiefly of the high style and interest of the preface, first of all, and the discrepancy inherent in the rest of the book accentuating the wide divergence between praiser and praised. It is James with reference to Brooke, it is not Henry

James informing of the young and handsome Rupert Brooke. Apollo in the flesh must do some mighty singing. Brooke had not done much of this when they laid him by on the borders of that farther sea. He had more to prove the heritage laid so heavily upon him by the unending host of his admirers and lovers. He needed relief from the popular notion, and we must relieve ourselves from his excessive popularity if we are to enjoy him rightly, by being just with him. A little time, and we should have learned his real distinction. It is too soon for us, and too late for him. We must accept him more for his finer indications then, and less for his achievement in the sense of mastery.

THE DEARTH OF CRITICS

THERE is just cause for wonder at the noticeable absence of critics in the field of painting, of individuals who are capable of some serious approach to the current tendencies in art. We have witnessed a very general failure to rise above the common or high-class reportorial level in this particular sphere. Why do so many people who write specifically about painting say so little that really relates to it? It is because most of them are journalists or men of letters who have made emotional excursions into this field, which is in most instances foreign to them; well-known literary artists, occasionally, intent upon varying their subject matter.

We read Meier-Graefe, for instance, on the development of modern art, and we find his analogies more or less stimulating, but taken as a whole his work is unsatisfactory from an artist's point of view; not much more than a sort of novel with art for its skeleton, or rather a handbook from which the untutored layman can gather superficial information about group and individual influences, a kind of verbal entertainment that is altogether wanting in true critical values. I have listened to lectures on art by people who were supposed to know about it, merely to see how much this type of critical study could satisfy the really artistic mind somewhat conversant with true relations, and I have found these lectures of but the slightest value, *resumés* compounded of wearisome and inappropriate detail. There is always an extreme lack of true definition, of true information, there is always too much of the amateur spirit passing for popular knowledge among these individuals who might otherwise do so much to form public taste and appreciation. Thus we find that even the chatty Meier-Graefe stops without going any further than Cézanne. It is possible that after writing two very heavy volumes upon the development of modern art, he has to remain silent on modern art itself, that he really feels he is not qualified to speak upon Cézanne and his successors; or does he assume possibly that there is nothing this side of Cézanne? How many writer people are there who really do understand what has taken place since then?

I have heard these characteristic remarks among the so-called art writers who write the regular notices for the daily journals—"You see I really don't know anything about the subject, but I have to write!" or—"I don't know anything about art, but I am reading up on it as much as possible so that I won't appear too stupid; for they send me out and I have to write something." Their attitude is the same as if their subject were a fire or a murder: but either of the latter would be much more in their line, calling for nothing but a registration of the simplest of facts. Just why these people have to write upon art will never be clear. But because of this altogether trivial relationship to the theme of painting we find it difficult to take seriously at all what we read in our dailies, in every case the barest notation with heavily worded comment, having little or no reference to what is important in the particular pictures themselves. How can anyone take these individuals seriously when they actually have no opinion to offer, and must rely either upon humor or indignation to inspire them?

If we turn to the pundits of criticism we find statements like this of Ruskin on Giotto:—"For all his use of opalescent warm color, Giotto is exactly like Turner, as in his swift expressional power he is like Gainsborough!" Again, speaking of Turner's *Fighting Téméraire,* he says: "Of all pictures of subjects not visibly involving human pain, this is, I believe, the most pathetic that was ever painted—no ruin was ever so affecting as this gliding of the vessel to her grave." Journalism of the first class certainly, but at the farthest stretch of the imagination how can one possibly think of Gainsborough or Turner in connection with any special quality of Giotto? As for the pathos of an aged ship, that belongs to poetry, as Coleridge has shown; sentiment of this kind has never had any proper place in painting. A far worthier type of appreciation in words is to be found, of course, in Pater's passages on *La Gioconda* and Botticelli's *Birth of Venus*. But these belong to a different realm, in which literature rises to a height independent of the pictures themselves by means of the suggestion that is in them, the power of suggestion being a finer alternative for crude and worthless description. We shall always dispute with the writer on art as to exactly what symbol is inherent in the presence of a rose in the hand or a tear upon the cheek, but we cannot quarrel when the matter is treated as sublimely as in the case of a literary artist like Pater. It is in the sphere of professed critical judgment that the literary authorities so often go astray.

Thus between the entertaining type of writer like Meier-Graefe and the daily reporter there is no middle ground. The journalist is frank and says that he doesn't know but that he must write; the other writes books that are well suited for reference purposes, but have scant bearing upon the actual truth in relation to pictures. Are there any critics who attempt seriously to approach the modern theme, who find it worth their while to go into modern esthetics with anything like sincerity or real earnestness of attitude? Only two that I am aware of. There is the intelligent Leo Stein, who seldom appears in print, but who makes an art of conversation on the subject; and there is Willard Huntington Wright, who has appeared extensively and certainly with intelligence also, both of these critical writers being very much at variance in theory, but both full of discernment whatever one may think of their individual ideas. We are sure of both as being thoroughly inside the subject, this theme of modern art, for they are somehow painter people. I even suspect them both of having once, like George Moore, painted seriously themselves.

Nevertheless there is a hopeful seriousness of interest developing in what is being done this side the sea, a rediscovery of native art of the sort that is occurring in all countries. The artist is being taught by means of war that there is no longer a conventional center of art, that the time-worn fetish of Paris as a necessity in his development has been dispensed with; and this is fortunate for the artist and for art in general. It is having its pronounced effect upon the creative powers of the individual in all countries, almost obliging him to create his own impulse upon his own soil; it is making the artist see that if he is really to create he must create irrespective of all that exists as convention in the mind.

How will this affect the artist? He will learn first of all to be concerned with himself, and what he puts forth of personality and of personal research will receive its character from his strict adherence to this principle, whether he proceeds by means of prevailing theories or by departure from them. The public will thus have no choice but to rely upon what he produces seriously as coming clearly from himself, from his own desire and labor. He will realize that it is not a trick, not a habit, not a trade—this modernity—and that with fashions it has nothing to do; that it is explicitly a part of our modern urge toward expression quite as much as the art of Corot and Millet were of Barbizon, as the art of Titian, Giorgione and Michelangelo were of Italy; that he and his time bear the strictest relationship to one another and that through this relationship he can best build up his own original power. Unable to depend therefore upon the confessedly untutored lay writer or even the better class essayist to tell him his place, he will establish himself, and his place will be determined in the régime of his day by precisely those qualities which he contributes to it. He will not rely too insistently upon idiosyncrasy; the failure of this we have already seen, in the post-impressionists.

The truth is that painters must sooner or later learn to express themselves in terms of pure language, they must learn that creation is the thing most expected of them, and, if possible, invention as well. Oddity in execution or idea is of the least importance. Artists have a more respectable service to perform than this dilettantist notion of beauty implies. Since the utter annihilation of sentimentality, of legend, of what we call poetry has taken place, a richer substance for expression has come to us by means of which the artist may express a larger, newer variety of matter, more relevant to our special need, our modernity.

THE DEARTH OF CRITICS

The war disintegrated the *art habit* and in this fact lies the hope of art. Fads have lost what slight interest they possessed, the folly of imitation has been exposed. As a result of this, I like to think that we shall have a finer type of expression, a richer kind of personal quality. Every artist is his own maker, his own liberator; he it is that should be the first to criticise, destroy and reconstruct himself, he should find no mood convenient, no attitude comfortable. What the lay-writer says of him in praise or blame will not matter so much in the future; he will respect first and last only those who have found the time to share his theme, at least in mind, if not in experience, and the discerning public will free itself from the temporary influences of the confessedly untutored critic. The artist will gain its confidence by reason of his own sincerity and intelligence. It is probable, too, that in time criticism in the mode of Ruskin will utterly disappear and the Meier-Graefe type of critic will have found a fitter and true successor, someone who, when he calls himself a critic, will prove a fairly clear title to the distinction and will not have to apologize for himself or for his occupation.

AFTERWORD

THE IMPORTANCE OF BEING "DADA"

WE are indebted to Tristan Tzara and his followers for the newest and perhaps the most important doctrinary insistence as applied to art which has appeared in a long time. Dada-ism is the latest phase of modernism in painting as well as in literature, and carries with it all the passion for freedom of expression which Marinetti sponsored so loudly in his futuristic manifestoes. It adds likewise an exhilarating quality of nihilism, imbibed, as is said, directly from the author of Zarathustra. Reading a fragment of the documentary statement of Dadaism, we find that the charm of the idea exists mainly in the fact that they wish all things levelled in the mind of man to the degree of commonplaceness which is typical of and peculiar to it.

Nothing is greater than anything else, is what the Dada believes, and this is the first sign of hope the artist at least can discover in the meaningless importance which has been invested in the term ART. It shows best of all that art is to betake itself on its own way blandly, despite the wish of its so ardent supporters and suppressors. I am greatly relieved as artist, to find there is at least one tenet I can hold to in my experience as a useful or a useless human being. I have always said for myself, I have no office, no obligations, no other "mission", dread-fullest of all words, than to find out the quality of humor that exists in experience, or life as we think we are entitled to call it. I have always felt the underlying fatality of habit in appreciation, because I have felt, and now actually more than ever in my existence, the fatality of habit indulged in by the artist. The artist has made a kind of subtle crime of his habitual expression, his emotional monotonies, and his intellectual inabilities.

If I announce on this bright morning that I am a "Dada-ist" it is not because I find the slightest need for, or importance in, a doctrine of any sort, it is only for convenience of myself and a few others that I take up the issue of adherence. An expressionist is one who expresses himself at all times in any way that is necessary and peculiar to him. A dada-ist is one who finds no one thing more important than any other one thing, and so I turn from my place in the scheme from expressionist to dada-ist with the easy grace that becomes any self-respecting humorist.

Having fussed with average intelligence as well as with average stupidity over the various dogmatic aspects of human experience such as art, religion, philosophy, ethics, morals, with a kind of obligatory blindness, I am come to the clearest point of my vision, which is nothing more or less than the superbly enlightening discovery that life as we know it is an essentially comic issue and cannot be treated other than with the spirit of comedy in comprehension. It is cause for riotous and healthy laughter, and to laugh at oneself in conjunction with the rest of the world, at one's own tragic vagaries, concerning the things one cannot name or touch or comprehend, is the best anodyne I can conjure in my mind for the irrelevant pains we take to impress ourselves and the world with the importance of anything more than the brilliant excitation of the moment. It is thrilling, therefore, to realize there is a healthy way out of all this dilemma of habit for the artist. One of these ways is to reduce the size of the "A" in art, to meet the size of the rest of the letters in one's speech. Another way is to deliver art from the clutches of its worshippers, and by worshippers I mean the idolaters and the commercialists of art. By the idolaters I mean those whose reverence for art is beyond their knowledge of it. By the commercialists I mean those who prey upon the ignorance of the unsophisticated, with pictures created by the esthetic habit of, or better to say, through the banality of, "artistic" temperament. Art is at present a species of vice in America, and it sorely and conspicuously needs prohibition or interference.

It is, I think, high time that those who have the artistic habit toward art should be apprised of the danger they are in in assuming of course that they hold vital interest in the development of intelligence. It is time therefore to interfere with stupidity in matters of taste and judgment. We learn little or nothing from habit excepting repetitive imitation. I should, for the benefit of you as reader, interpose here a little information from the mind of Francis Picabia, who was until the war conspicuous among the cubists, upon the subject of dada-ism.

"Dada smells of nothing, nothing, nothing.
It is like your hopes: nothing.
Like your paradise: nothing.
Like your idols: nothing.
Like your politicians: nothing.
Like your heroes: nothing.
Like your artists: nothing.
Like your religions: nothing."

A litany like this coming from one of the most notable dada-ists of the day, is too edifying for proper expression. It is like a window opened upon a wide cool place where all parts of one's exhausted being may receive the kind of air that is imperative to it. For the present, we may say, a special part of one's being which needs the most and the freshest air is that chamber in the brain where art takes hold and flourishes like a bed of fungus in the dark.

What is the use, then, of knowing anything about art until we know precisely what it is? If it is such an orchidaceous rarity as the world of worshippers would have us believe, then we know it must be the parasitic equivalent of our existence feeding upon the health of other functions and sensibilities in ourselves. The question comes why worship what we are not familiar with? The war has taught us that idolatry is a past virtue and can have no further place with intelligent people living in the present era, which is for us the only era worth consideration. I have a hobby-horse therefore—to ride away with, out into the world of intricate common experience; out into the arena with those who know what the element of life itself is, and that I have become an expression of the one issue in the mind worth the consideration of the artist, namely fluidic change. How can anything to which I am not related, have any bearing upon me as artist? I am only dada-ist because it is the nearest I have come to scientific principle in experience. What yesterday can mean is only what yesterday was, and tomorrow is something I cannot fathom until it occurs. I ride my own hobby-horse away from the dangers of art which is with us a modern vice at present, into the wide expanse of magnanimous diversion from which I may extract all the joyousness I am capable of, from the patterns I encounter.

The same disgust which was manifested and certainly enjoyed by Duse, when she demanded that the stage be cleared of actors in order to save the creative life of the stage, is the same disgust that makes us yearn for wooden dolls to make abstract movements in order that we may release art from its infliction of the big "A", to take away from art its pricelessness and make of it a new and engaging diversion, pastime, even dissipation if you will; for all real expression is a phase of dissipation in itself: To release art from the disease of little theatre-ism,

and from the mandibles of the octopus-like worshipper that eats everything, in the line of spurious
estheticism within range, disgorging it without intelligence or comprehension upon the consciousness
of the not at all stupid public, with a so obviously
pernicious effect.

"Dada is a fundamentally religious attitude,
analogous to that of the scientist with his eyeglass
glued to the microscope." Dada is irritated by those
who write "Art, Beauty, Truth", with capital letters,
and who make of them entities superior to man.
"Dada scoffs at capital letters, atrociously." "Dada
ruining the authority of constraints, tends to set free
the natural play of our activities." "Dada therefore
leads to amoralism and to the most spontaneous and
consequently the least logical lyricism. This lyricism
is expressed in a thousand ways of life." "Dada
scrapes from us the thick layers of filth deposited
on us by the last few centuries." "Dada destroys,
and stops at that. Let Dada help us to make a complete clearance, then each of us rebuild a modern
house with central heating, and everything to the
drain, Dadas of 1920."

Remembering always that Dada means hobby-
horse, you have at last the invitation to make merry
for once in our new and unprecedented experience
over the subject of ART with its now reduced front
letter. It is the newest and most admirable reclaimer
of art in that it offers at last a release for the expression of natural sensibilities. We can ride away

to the radiant region of "Joie de Vivre", and find that life and art are one and the same thing, resembling each other so closely in reality, that it is never a question of whether it shall or must be set down on paper or canvas, or given any greater degree of expression than we give to a morning walk or a pleasant bath, or an ordinary rest in the sunlight.

Art is then a matter of how one is to take life now, and not by any means a matter of how the Greeks or the Egyptians or any other race has shown it to be for their own needs and satisfaction. If art was necessary to them, it is unnecessary to us now, therefore it is free to express itself as it will. You will find, therefore, that if you are aware of yourself, you will be your own perfect dada-ist, in that you are for the first time riding your own hobby-horse into infinity of sensation through experience, and that you are one more satisfactory vaudevillian among the multitudes of dancing legs and flying wits. You will learn after all that the bugaboo called LIFE is a matter of the tightrope and that the stars will shine their frisky approval as you glide, if you glide sensibly, with an eye on the fun in the performance. That is what art is to be, must come to in the consciousness of the artist most of all, he is perhaps the greatest offender in matters of judgment and taste; and the next greatest offender is the dreadful go-between or "middleman" esthete who so glibly contributes effete values to our present day conceptions.

ADVENTURES IN THE ARTS

We must all learn what art really is, learn to relieve it from the surrounding stupidities and from the passionate and useless admiration of the horde of false idolaters, as well as the money changers in the temple of success. Dada-ism offers the first joyous dogma I have encountered which has been invented for the release and true freedom of art. It is therefore most welcome since it will put out of use all heavy hands and light fingers in the business of art and set them to playing a more honourable and sportsmanlike game. We shall learn through dada-ism that art is a witty and entertaining pastime, and not to be accepted as our ever present and stultifying affliction.

93